GW00738204

Dialogue with Hans Küng

Dialogue with Hans Küng

Walter Jens and
Karl-Josef Kuschel

with
Hans Küng's Farewell Lecture

SCM PRESS LTD

Translated by John Bowden from the German
*Dialog mit Hans Küng. Mit der
Abschiedsvorlesung von Hans Küng,*
published 1996 by Piper Verlag, Munich

0 334 02674 1

First published 1997 by
SCM Press Ltd
9–17 St Albans Place London N1 0NX

Typeset by Regent Typesetting, London
Printed in Great Britain by Biddles Ltd,
Guildford and King's Lynn

Contents

Contents

For Marianne Sauer,
in friendship

An Explanation

An open dialogue with Hans Küng has not happened very often. There has been much polemic, much repudiation from the perspective of a dogmatism claiming to be orthodox which is sure that it is right, and a good deal of dissociation, with the slogan 'He's no longer a Catholic'. But conversation in solidarity with Hans Küng has been much rarer. The present book attempts to engage in this, aiming at a critical dialogue which seeks to understand him on the basis of a thorough knowledge of his extensive writings and with respect for his academic life's work.

The texts printed here were given as lectures in the University of Tübingen on the occasion of Hans Küng's retirement in February 1996. They have been brought together as a book which shows through Küng's works that central theological questions have lost nothing of their vitality and existential importance.

Tübingen, May 1996

Walter Jens   Karl-Josef Kuschel

KARL-JOSEF KUSCHEL

Theology in Freedom. Basic Dimensions of the Theology of Hans Küng

The horizon

I begin with two scenes. The first is set in Rome, in 1928.

On 6 January of that year, the year in which Hans Küng was born, Pope Pius XI published a new encyclical under the title *Mortalium animos*, which once again laid down the fundamental attitude of the Catholic Church towards ecumenism. The occasion for it was the flourishing ecumenical movement in world Protestantism. This had caused deep unrest: evidently 'many Catholics' had also been 'attracted and enthused' by the cause of ecumenism; they hoped that in this way they could contribute to the unity of the churches. But this was said to be 'a grave error', which destroyed the foundation of the Catholic faith. No, for Catholics it continued to be the case that all Christians could be united only by the return to the Catholic Church, which alone brought salvation, of the churches of the Reformation which had broken away through their own fault. As Pius XI put it: 'Lamentably, the children have left their paternal home . . . May they return again to their common father, who has long forgotten the wrong that they have done to the Apostolic See and will accept them with a loving heart.'[1]

The second scene is also set in Rome, at an ordination to the priesthood, in October 1954.

Like all those who were to become priests, before his ordination the twenty-six-year-old Hans Küng also had to swear the 'anti-modernist oath' which was introduced in 1910 by Pius X:

I embrace and accept each and everything that is defined, proposed and declared by the infallible teaching authority of the Church, and in particular those principal truths which are directly opposed to the errors of this time. [There follows an enumeration of the errors in eleven articles, which ends:] Thus I hold, and shall continue to hold to my last breath, the faith of the Fathers in the sure charism of truth that is, has been and always will be in the succession of the bishops from the apostles, for the purpose that not what seems better and more suited according to the culture of each age should be held, but that the absolute and immutable truth, which from the beginning was preached by the apostles, 'should never be believed, never be understood in a different way'. I promise that I shall keep all this faithfully, wholly and sincerely, never deviating from it in teaching or in any way in word or in writing. Thus I promise, thus I swear; so help me God and these holy gospels of God.[2]

This was probably the eighth time that Küng swore this oath, since candidates for the priesthood in Rome were compelled to swear it a number of times during the

course of their study. Nor was it the last time, since professors of theology also had to swear this oath, which
was officially abolished only in 1967.

The anti-ecumenical encyclical and the anti-modernist
oath are only particularly striking crystallizations of
a Catholic anti-ecumenism and anti-modernism which
indicate the kind of world from which Hans Küng's
theology developed. It is the world of the 'Counter
Reformation Anti-Modernist Paradigm of the Middle
Ages', the fascination and contradictions of which Küng
was able to perceive later more acutely than almost anyone else.[3] I do not want to consider Hans Küng's theology in isolation here, but to regard it as far as possible
as representative of a whole generation of theologians,
a generation which had to dismantle the bastions of
Roman traditionalism in order to free Catholic theology
for true catholicity.[4]

We should have no doubts about it: for many Catholic
theologians sensitive to scientific and cultural changes,
above all the first half of this century meant theology
not in freedom but in anxiety. Anyone who was not
engaged in neo-scholastic Denziger theology or who did
not delight in the positivism of the magisterium but was
open to the challenge of historicism, the criticism of
religions and secular culture, was open to the suspicion
of being a 'modernist'. Hardly any of the pioneering,
innovative Catholic theologians of the time was not
dogged by a lifelong anxiety about being disciplined by
the magisterium. One example is Romano Guardini,
who in his younger years as a theology student in
Tübingen found himself involved in the controversy
over modernism embodied in the figure of the Tübingen
theologian Wilhelm Koch.[5] At that time Koch was being

5

disciplined, and according to Karl Rahner, this 'caused Guardini a trauma which never completely disappeared for the rest of his career'. He 'kept out of any involvement in possible conflicts' and 'always somewhat anxiously avoided' dogmatic questions.[6] Not to mention Karl Rahner himself, who had been subjected to censorship by his order in the 1950s under pressure from Rome. Or Teilhard de Chardin, also a Jesuit, who was silenced by a ban on publishing and was ostracized within the church. Or Yves Congar, the Dominican, the leading intellectual of the 'Nouvelle théologie' in France, who was banished from his country and exiled to Jerusalem. Or . . .

Is all this a thing of the past? More recent public statements by Catholic theologians, culminating in the 1989 Cologne Declaration, show how little has changed. The Declaration has a significant title which could be translated: 'No to Paternalistic Control – Yes to an Open Catholicity'. This text, which was pioneered by the Tübingen Catholic theologians Norbert Greinacher and Dietmar Mieth, is a document of theological self-respect. Moreover it was signed by another 160 Catholic professors of theology in the German-speaking countries and in the Netherlands. Similar declarations followed in Belgium, France, Spain, Italy, Brazil and the USA. Also in 1989 the Tübingen Catholic theologian Peter Hünermann spoke of a 'third great crisis of modernism',[7] in which, he argued, we found ourselves in the pontificate of John Paul II – referring back to the two previous crises under Pius XI in the middle of the last century and since 1907 under Pius X (the encyclical *Pascendi*).

Against this background we can understand better the tragi-comic tone of the anecdote with which thirty-two years ago, in 1964, Hans Küng began his ceremonial address on the subject of freedom at the opening of the Institute for Ecumenical Research: 'The Church and Freedom? "Very interesting," was the comment, said with a charming smile, by a friendly colleague of mine from a famous American university: "I know there's a church, and I know there's freedom, but I didn't know that you could have the church and freedom together." '[8] No wonder that such a climate gives rise to what Peter Sloterdijk in his *Critique of Cynical Reason* called 'religious cynicism': the tactic of disguising one's own thoughts, the split into private and public which makes a person a rebel in private but a conformist in public. Not without a mock-cynical regret, Sloterdijk produced the following analysis: 'In the conditions of the modern world, one really has to learn how to be a Catholic ... Poor Hans Küng. After such brilliant studies he should have realized that the Catholic way of being intelligent is rewarding only if people also know how to hide decently the fact that they know too much.'[9]

But why does this cynical statement fail to penetrate to Hans Küng's basic attitude? Why was his way of being both Catholic and intelligent combined with public controversy? Why did Sloterdijk's dictum about decently hiding the fact that one knows too much not apply to him so evidently as a comment by the American exegete John McKenzie, who in connection with the infallibility debate once wrote: 'Hans Küng on *Infallibility*? This Tiger is not Discreet'?[10] In short, why did this indiscreet 'tiger' not become a religious cynic, like other Catholic theologians of his generation, who like him argued for another way of being Catholic, beyond conformist assimilation and cynically dismissive laughs?

7

Karl-Josef Kuschel

The centre

One answer is that there is a centre to this theology, a truth which forms the foundation for its freedom and from this freedom develops the boldness to be a Christian, even in conflict with the permissive spirit of the time on the one hand and the demon of authoritarianism within the church on the other. This truth is described with the basic theological term 'the justification of the sinner'. Anyone who, like Hans Küng as early as his 1957 dissertation (on Karl Barth), has understood the meaning of justification by God through grace alone at the deepest level, not only intellectually as the doctrine of justification but also existentially as an invitation to radical trust in the God who is always greater, more mysterious and more gracious, can understand the encouraging stream of warmth which this message emanates.[11]

For the statement about the justification of the sinner formulates the basic conviction that the Christian has only one main concern: to give God alone the glory, and not to give it to anything or anyone else. The Christian's concern is to give the glory to a God who in incomprehensible freedom chooses a people, the people of Israel (for the salvation of all peoples), a God who justifies the godless in Jesus Christ and who expects nothing from human beings but unconditional trust. In Küng, a theology of freedom grows out of commitment to this truth. Truth is the foundation of freedom.

Anyone whose thought is based on this truth knows self-critically that human beings cannot achieve anything before God, no matter how much devotion they show to the church, no matter how many volumes of

8

theology they write. Nor can they achieve anything by pious asceticism or an acutely brilliant intellect. And at the same time, as a criticism of the church as an institution this means: 'Where the Spirit of the Lord is, there is freedom' (II Cor. 3.17). However, freedom is not understood in modern terms as stubborn autonomy or unlimited independence, but in biblical terms as liberated freedom (Gal. 5.1), which becomes concrete in a spirituality and praxis of withstanding and resisting – according to a saying of the apostle to the Gentiles:

> For I am sure that neither death, nor life, nor angels, nor principalities, nor things present, nor things to come, nor powers, nor height, nor depth, nor anything else in all creation, will be able to separate us from the love of God in Christ Jesus our Lord (Rom. 8.38f.).

It is striking how often this key text from Romans appears already in the early writings of Hans Küng, as a statement which at a very early stage indicates that here a theologian is arming himself spiritually for future controversies in theology and church because he does not want to be one of those silent figures who buy their clear conscience by looking the other way . . .

Five dimensions

Five basic dimensions of Hans Küng's theology can be understood better on the basis of this central truth, on which he often reflects and which is even more often tacitly presupposed. For the message of the justification of the godless serves directly or indirectly, all through his life as a theologian, as a basis for:

1. A critical location of the Christian in the world;

2. A Christian identity in the light of historical-critical consciousness;
3. A liberation of the Catholic for true catholicity;
4. An ecumenical reconciliation between the Christian churches;
5. A dialogical existence with the non-Christian religions.

I shall go on to comment as far as I can in a short space on these five dimensions.

Dimension 1. The critical location of the Christian in the world

With all due respect, today's Emeritus has always looked enviably worldly, always rather more athletic than average, always somewhat slimmer and more tanned. He does not seem to despise the good things in life. And I would bet that statistically the most frequent reason why people are amazed at Hans Küng is because such a person is a Catholic theologian. He does not look like one . . .

But I would recommend all those who confuse a tanned face laboriously acquired from the sunshine with frivolity to share a working day with Hans Küng – as Walter Jens once did.[12] Anyone who has not yet discovered what a work ethic is will certainly learn it at his side. Here theological work is done on the principle of making difficulties for oneself: the problems are not there to be left aside, but to be tackled.

However, my concern here is not just to show respect for a hard work ethic. My basic question here is that of the relationship between worldliness and Christianity, and this question touches on the moral substance of our theological existence. How can anyone be a Christian theologian and indeed a priest, with the security of a state university, in a position to enjoy the good things of bourgois life, without ever having asked whether one's life-style still corresponds to that of a disciple of Christ, or whether it does not fall short of this?

From an early stage Hans Küng had one particular model in reflecting on the relationship between worldliness and Christianity: Sir Thomas More, the Lord Chancellor of England, who was murdered under King Henry VIII as a martyr of conscience. One has only to read the early work of Hans Küng on *Freedom in the World. Sir Thomas More* (1964), to find the question raised directly. According to the New Testament, do not poverty, celibacy and obedience go with Christian perfection? In order to live in accordance with the gospel, is one not called to renounce possessions, the enjoyment of beautiful things, the use of anything that is pleasant and convenient, and to show solidarity with the humiliated and the sufferers – even in one's life-style? Has one not to give up everything in order not to be suspected of conformity?

At the same time, however, there is this strange worldly saint Thomas More. This rich, successful and powerful man could enjoy his possessions; his family and the state meant a great deal to him; as a man of the world he could enjoy the good things of life. But all this stood under a proviso, that no form of life should be absolutized, that in every form of life one should ultimately be orientated on the will of God. Property, yes, but without becoming its slave; family and public power, yes, but without making them idols; the good things of life, yes, but without ever setting one's heart on them. So Thomas More attempts to live out discipleship of Christ as a man of God, ready to let go of everything that matters for God. 'A man for all seasons', from whom one can learn what a Christian man must do in an emergency . . .

Did the life-style of this man of the world and later saint accord with scripture, Hans Küng asks in his short book, reflecting on his own situation? By way of an answer he refers to the worldly apostle Paul's doctrine of charisms, and this moreover is in fact the key to an adequate locating of the Christian in the world: 'There are varieties of gifts but the same Spirit; and there are varieties of service, but the same Lord . . . All these are inspired by one and the same spirit who apportions to each one individually as he wills' (12.4f., 11).

What this means is that Paul does not legalize a single Christian form of life, but sees gifts of the Spirit – possibilities for following Christ – in all forms of life. So even Paul need not renounce the possibilities of the world in a pessimistic asceticism, but can make use of them. Nothing need be alien to a Christian. Christians can be content with any situation, and 'know how to be abased and know how to abound' (Phil. 4.12). Why? Because 'in the Spirit' – thus Küng, interpreting Paul – a Christian can show 'the over-riding detachment of a free man, which makes him, in the last analysis, indifferent to abundance and to want'.[13] Active indifference to everything is the decisive key word. And from this basic attitude both the life of the Christian and a worldly life are possible in a complex bourgeois society: discipleship of Christ beyond denying the world and conforming with it.

At the same time, here is a Christian who from this same centre is able to see round the blinkers of a society of which he himself is a part. For the first time in Küng's works, his book *On Being a Christian* contains a critical analysis of the modern competitive society.[14] It does not follow a simple class scheme but rather an analysis (enlightened by the Christian ethos) of the inhumanities immanent in this society at *all* levels. At *all* levels it is true that the value of humanity is increasingly rated in terms of success, reputation and income. Human beings are often thought important by other human beings only in terms of what they achieve, in terms of the functional contribution that they make. I am grateful to Hans Küng since *On Being a Christian* for providing a decisive theological counterpoint in which the message of justification finds a political and social focus: before God, human beings are more than their achievements and successes. Life is given meaning by God, even when it is lacking in achievement, even in misfortune, even in failure and even in bodily decay.

We need to note how the analysis of society in *On Being a Christian* is continued later in *Global Responsibility* (1991). The decisive difference is that now paradigm analysis provides the necessary theory within the framework of which the effects of epoch-making revolutions in human social life can be diagnosed more precisely. Here Küng joins in the complex debate over a theory of modernity. What Jürgen Habermas has called the 'uncompleted project of modernity' is not simply rejected or taken forward, but analysed critically.[15] Here is a perception, above all, of the immanent destructiveness of modernity through a faith in science, technology and economics, making modernity degenerate into inhumanity and godlessness. This is the context of the project of a global ethic. The diagnosis of our time and its culture presupposed here is not pessimistic, but soberly empirical.

This diagnosis finds that a basic ethical orientation, the formation of an elementary conscience and moral standards, are gradually disappearing all over the world in similar conditions of civilization, economics and technology. Often there is the threat of ethics being replaced by aesthetics: what gives pleasure is permissible, and pleasure is 'What pleases me'. This is a global phenomenon in which all cultures and religions are involved. Everywhere men and women allow themselves a morality with diminished and movable criteria, renouncing all too long-term, even life-long loyalties, and attaching the proviso of self-fulfilment to every risk, insisting on the right to go back on any commitment and indifferent to any wider consensus.[16]

It is here that for Küng the traditional religions, and in particular the Christian churches, also have an indispensable function: as spiritual and moral forces they withstand the particular spirit of the time and hold up before society a mirror in which the decline in values is seen to triumph at the cost of ideals; greed for private enrichment to triumph at the expense of the common good; and increasingly refined amusements provided by the experience industry to triumph in favour of a lowering of the threshold of shame. Here is a society in which – unnoticed by many people – a great confusion has come about: living standards are already regarded as the meaning of life. Here the 'global ethic' project stems from a basic notion: an ethic inspired by religion, rightly understood, is not a pious veneer on a society which in other respects can go its own way, pursuing its business and amusements forgetful of morality. Rather, an ethic anchored in belief in God entails the freedom to accept responsibility for one's fellow human being, to commit oneself to ideals and to be ready for sacrifice for the well-being of the whole. According to a saying of Gandhi which Küng is so fond of quoting: 'The Ganges of rights rises from the Himalaya of duties' . . .

Dimension 2. A Christian identity in the light of historical-critical consciousness

Hans Küng has often reported how neo-scholastic dogmatics, the ideological support of the Roman system, has done everything possible to obliterate every trace of historicity from the development of the church. Church teaching and praxis are presented as if they were eternal and immutable: always the same; everywhere the same; the same teachings accepted by all . . . Moreover, according to traditional theology the Roman system with the Pope at its head is said to have achieved a degree of perfection which requires obedience, admiration and sympathy, not critical questioning. So it must have seemed like a liberation when the younger generation of theologians at that time experienced the demythologizing of the Roman system through the discovery of its historicity. What had claimed to be original and eternal was in reality often merely the product of mediaeval Roman centralism, the anti-Protestant Counter-Reformation or the anti-modernist nineteenth century.

The problem went far beyond mere church reform. It became really acute when this generation of theologians came up against the historical-critical exegesis practised in the sphere of liberal Protestantism. For them, too, this raised a disturbing question which still keeps Christian theology on edge: the question of origins as the critical norm of truth. If a paradigm shift in Catholic theology was due anywhere, it was at this point: taking seriously the original form of the church as a critical criterion for the church as it really exists.

Hans Küng already took up this question in his book *The Church* (1967), and it continues down to the analysis of paradigms in his *Christianity* (1995). What is the Christian message? In its essentials, and at the deepest level, it has once again to be radically distinguished from the many forms which Christianity has produced in the course of its history. Here Küng does not replace the historical hermeneutic of the Catholic tradition by which the church organically achieves perfection with a liberal Protestant hermeneutic of decadence. In other words, for Küng the kingdom of God and the church are by no means played off against each other in a pattern of light and shade, climax and decline. For Küng, church history is neither a history of decay nor a criminal history. Rather, for anyone who believes in the promise of the presence of the spirit of Christ in the world and the church 'always, to the end of the world' (Matt. 28.20), church history is the ever-new establishment of the essential *in* and *despite* the inessential. Therefore according to Küng, church history must constantly be re-written critically in the light of a history of Christianity, precisely because the church's historical establishment of itself at *all* levels produced not only loyalty to the gospel but also betrayal of the gospel.

However, Hans Küng has never left any doubt that the church has an indestructible 'essence', an immortal 'soul', an inexhaustible spiritual 'source of energy'. His answer is as disarming as it is basic, and only the excessive complexity of Catholic dogmatics as it has grown up in history, and a historically unprecedented crisis in the pastoral acceptance of church teaching, explains why this generation of theologians once again began to long for it to be possible to present the Christian faith in an elementary form in 'short formulae'. The answer was: what is Christian is not identical with just any eternal idea, any high dogma, any moral principle, but is identical with a specific person in history. Contrary to all the clichés of the critics, for Küng this does not simply mean the 'Jesus of history' as reconstructed by historians; what he means is, rather, the event of Jesus Christ as it originally shines out in the New Testament in a characteristic mixture of history and preaching. So the essence of Christianity is not simply the 'historical Jesus', but Jesus of Nazareth, as the Lord who is irreplaceable in history and at the same time universally present in the Spirit: Jesus the Jew, who is proclaimed as the Messiah for Israel and the Kyrios for the world.

No generation of Catholic theologians has ever shown such passion for historicity in this key question as that of Hans Küng. When this passion entered twentieth-century Catholic theology from modern Protestantism, it developed an unprecedented creativity there. The quest for Jesus? After centuries of unquestioned doctrine about Christ a new question arose. What did Jesus really want? After centuries of apparently assured dogmatics, there was a new amazement. What is special about this man, the man from Nazareth, which has not been established once and for all by a church which has really existed for two thousand years? What is his mystery, which has not already been 'grasped' with age-old formulae and interpreted to the last detail? So over against all the theological surveys, there is a new acceptance of the pulsing life of a person who cannot be domesticated, who cannot be controlled by the church, who cannot be grasped by theology, and cannot be assigned a place in the history of religions . . .

One core of Küng's theology is the way in which he has been affected by the figure of Jesus of Nazareth. He constantly wants to bring this man, Jesus of Nazareth, to light: his surprisingly liberating message of good news for humankind; his career, which was unusually rapid and full of conflict; his dramatic fate of passion, cross, resurrection. Indeed, we shall only understand Küng's theology if we describe it as the only attempt without any historical reductionism to find a scholarly home in theology for the one question: 'Would Jesus have understood this?' 'What if he returned?' This unrest, characteristic of Dostoievsky, can also be traced in the work of Hans Küng: he is driven by the basic notion of what it means today to correspond to Jesus – in church and society.

So many passages in Küng's writings are written in the form 'I cannot imagine that'; they are driven by a passion to look at the situation in church and society with the ideas of Christ *redivivus*. Such passages read like this:

When I think of the Church of the future I cannot with the best will in the world imagine that the One whom Christianity invokes would, if he returned, take a position on today's controversial questions like that of the Roman, and often the German, church authorities;
– that he who warned the Pharisees about placing

intolerable burdens on people's shoulders would today declare all 'artificial' contraception a moral sin;

- that he who was continually accompanied by women (his support system) and every one of whose apostles – with the exception of Paul – was and remained married would in today's situation forbid marriage to ordained men and ordination to all women;
- that he would in this way increasingly rob the communities of their chaplains and pastors and would offer them substitute eucharists;
- that he who took the adulterers and sinners under his wing would issue such harsh verdicts on delicate questions and issues that have to be judged in a nuanced and critical fashion, such as premarital intercourse, homosexuality and abortion . . .

No, I just cannot think that if he had returned today he would have agreed

- when in the ecumenical area confessional differences are upheld as an impediment to marriage, indeed have really been made an impediment to entrance into pastoral service for Catholic lay theologians (as they are for Protestant aspirants to the ministry);
- when the validity of the ordination and eucharistic celebrations of Protestant pastors was contested;
- when open communion and joint eucharistic celebrations, the common building of churches and parish centres, and ecumenical religious instruction were prevented;
- when instead of convincing Catholic theologians,

student pastors, teachers of religion, journalists, association officials, and other responsible persons by giving reasons, Church authorities tried to tame them with decrees, 'declarations', and depriving them of their canonical mission . . . [17]

However, no textbook theology could ever match the liveliness of a person. The theological content needed a new literary figure. Moreover with *On Being a Christian*, in Küng's case too, something unique came into being in the genre of theological books: a carefully thought out synthesis made up of narration and reflection. Here historical criticism prevents any naiveté in the narration. But what is then told, has to be told, as dramatic history, shows that this theologian has not 'grasped' a figure like Jesus. For him the figure of Jesus remains enigmatic, uncanny, mysterious. Ultimately – despite all efforts to know him – Jesus escapes any conceptuality. Moreover, his mystery is also that of the incomprehensible God himself.[18]

It is the same in the book *Does God Exist?*. This chooses in its approach to God the career of four philosophical thinkers in which the struggle over the question of God is dramatically played out in all its heights and in all its depths. And at the same time it is an argumentative discussion of the possibility of responding intellectually to belief in God in modern times.

Anyone who embarks on these chapters will discover an experimental theology, committed to the riddles of life, alive to the process by which human faith ferments. And the literary form for this experimental theology is no longer the dogmatic textbook but exploration by means of individual studies. Here we have a writer who makes proposals, shows possible solutions in a Brechtian way.

That perhaps explains why in the dispute with the magisterium anxiety arose above all over Küng's christology. Does he still believe as the church does? Is anything still binding for him? Does he still have an assured faith? Here what was left out of account was the centre from which all Küng's sketches of christology come: the fact that in any decisive confession before the incomprehensible and ineffable God there are no human securities. The risk of faith remains, and on earth cannot be removed by any authority. And because this is the case, for Küng, too, the use of the methods of historical criticism is, as it is for Bultmann, the application of the doctrine of justification. For such a theology has understood that no church tradition may be made an idol and that the mystery of the living God ultimately escapes all that theologians can say.

Dimension 3. A liberation of the Catholic for true catholicity

Anyone for whom the essentials of what is Christian are identical with its original form gains the freedom to examine all the structures which have grown up in history to that effect, to see whether they have still preserved the original freedom of the forms of Christian faith and life. Such a person gains courage to tell his church – to the point of getting on the nerves of all those involved: 'Have courage to let go again of whatever is not part of its original essence. Let go of cultural and historical elements which have come to be attached to this essence. Above all have the courage to let go of whatever makes the message incredible because it nips the spirit of freedom in the bud.'

For Hans Küng, this too is the application of the message of justification. And those who do not see this centre will always reduce his criticism of the church to the psychological dimension: to quarrelsomeness, posturing and intellectual arrogance. But if at its deepest level the message of justification means that nothing and no one can force a way between human beings and God; that nothing and no one can manipulate God's gracious concern for the sinner, not even the church and its ordained ministry, bishop and pope; that everything which constitutes the church has the sole function of serving before God – then this message creates freedom for constantly new changes in the church and its theology which are brought about by the Spirit (including the necessary change in the person of the theologian concerned). And at the same time it ensures that no legitimate criticism turns into cynical and dismissive laughter, because it is certain that the essence of what is Christian is indestructible, despite all failure and misuse.

There is a little anecdote that I cannot get out of my mind in this connection. In the 1960s Hans Küng had a private visit from a cardinal (there were others at that time). The cardinal stayed over the weekend, and the question of worship arose. The two men quickly agreed not to go to the local church in order to avoid public attention. Küng suggested a domestic liturgy. They could sit together at the table and celebrate the eucharist there. The cardinal was confused and asked uncertainly, 'Just like *that*?' '*Just like* that?' Küng asked in reply, 'Did Jesus do more?' And the cardinal sat down at the dining table.

This anecdote demonstrates clearly what the degeneration of what is Christian means – in contrast to all the excessive complexity of liturgy, canon law or dogmatics. The uncertain question of the confused cardinal conveys the astonishment of all those who think that the essence of what is Christian has been shattered once a concrete form has been abandoned. However, finding a way back to the great simplicity of the Christian message is not to be confused with a reductive simplification or theological populism, but is the preservation of what is decisive and essential. A reduction of complexity – yes, but not in a regressive way: that is the key in Küng's concern to assert again, in faithfulness to the origins, what being a Christian means for men and women of our time.

One example is the rehabilitation of heretics. Anyone who has ever been horrified by the degree of repression with which the truth has been imposed within the church; anyone who has seen how often in history heretics have been produced who later enjoyed rehabilitation in the church, will also have recognized how often the history of the establishment of the truth has been a history of the victors, which later had to be rewritten as a history of self-deception.[19] One experience I shall never forget is that of reading Küng's chapters on 'The Church and the Jews' and 'The Church and the Heretics' in his 1967 book on *The Church*, and the chapters still make a deep impression on me. I shall never forget my first encounter with them, because these chapters brought home to me as a young student for the first time in all its acuteness the self-critical question of a Christian theologian about a history of the church's guilt, extending over many centuries, in respect of both Jews and heretics, which almost amounted to a question of theodicy:

We may wonder how this centuries-long history of horrors, of suffering and death, culminating in the murder of millions by the Nazis, could come about . . . We ask this question here simply as Christians, as members of a community which distinguished itself from the old people of God by calling itself the new people of God. How could all this happen? Shame and guilt must be our silent reply – would we wish to speak above the enforced silence of millions?[20]

And what about the heretics? Here a Catholic theologian puts an end to a black-and-white apologetic directed against heretics which had been practised for centuries as a matter of course. In Küng we can suddenly read of 'truth in heresy', indeed of 'error in the church', and of the 'good faith of the heretics' and 'violent proceedings' against them from which 'the main command of love has been excluded'. Sentences like this are still stamped on my memory (and my copy of the first edition *The Church* has written in it: 'never forget page 302'):

Few things harmed the Church and its unity so much as the violent treatment of heretics, the evidence of a lack of love which made countless people doubt the truth and drove them out of the church. The road to 'pure doctrine' cannot be driven over corpses. Zealous faith must not be perverted into doctrinaire intolerance. It is only a little step from 'orthodoxy' to that blind and ruthless fanaticism which is the very soul of all inquisitions. However many historical and psychological explanations may be found for the Inquisition, no possible justification for it can be found when we set it beside the Gospel of Jesus Christ. A Church deserts the Gospel at the point where it tries to liquidate all opposition by physical or spiritual murder, and makes a communion of love into a religion of executioners.[21]

Jürgen Moltmann once spoke of the 'honour of theology' in connection with the heretic Giordano Bruno, namely doing everything possible to restore the dignity of this man who was excommunicated and burned at the stake.[22] In fact every new generation of theologians, for the sake of its own honour, is called critically to examine former condemnations in the light of new insights and to correct them decisively where necessary. Decisive consequences are to be drawn from the history of the dialectic of truth and error for a different way of dealing with dissent within the church. The Tübingen Protestant theologian Eberhard Jüngel made some apt remarks about this in 1980, arising out of what was happening at the time:

The freedom of theology also includes that courage for the truth which dares to distinguish right teaching from false teaching . . . But in every instance the 'No' in the name of truth will have as its criterion of authenticity the fact that it is accompanied by the 'Yes' of love. We do not know that the apostle Paul withdrew the *missio canonica* from the apostle Peter because he had to resist the latter to the face for the sake of the truth of the Gospel. Love is the key element in the freedom for which the truth of the gospel must be freed, and in which constantly new questions must be asked about precisely this truth.[23]

And because that is the case, because love is the key element for freedom, we cannot keep silent about the injustice which is still waiting for reparation: the denial of the *missio canonica* to Hans Küng and his exclusion from his Catholic Theological Faculty in Tübingen. It is time seriously to set about the rehabilitation of Hans Küng as a Catholic theologian, both canonically and theologically, since his rehabilitation 'from below' has not only never suffered, but has increased over the course of the past years. The Austrian and German 'plebiscites' are the most visible sign of this.

The basis for clarifying the theological questions of substance which are in dispute has been provided by the Catholic theologians of note who appeared in the 930-page *Festschrift* for Hans Küng published in 1993. My fellow-editor Hermann Häring and I used the results of these studies as the occasion to make a public appeal, which I repeat here:

We request the Bishop of Rottenburg-Stuttgart to initiate proceedings for the revision of the measures which were taken against Hans Küng by his predecessor in December 1979 under strong pressure from Rome. Such a measure would not only undo a historical injustice but also give a sign of the consistent renewal of the church in the spirit of the Second Vatican Council.[24]

Happily this appeal has now also been taken up by the present Catholic Faculty of Theology in Tübingen, which Hans Küng was compelled to leave in 1980. In a statement read aloud publicly on 12 February 1996 by the dean of this faculty on the occasion of Hans Küng's retirement, a statement which was supported by the overwhelming majority of the faculty, the 'complete rehabilitation of Hans Küng' was called for. This is what the statement said:

The Catholic Faculty of Theology neither caused nor implemented the departure of Hans Küng in 1979 and it regrets the developments of that time. Without passing judgment on those events, the faculty would like to continue its efforts as far as possible to maintain links with Hans Küng. This has already happened so far through the dissertations and habilitations which he has supervised in our faculty. Two *extraordinarius* professors and a lecturer in our faculty are his pupils ... Hans Küng has always developed his questions and theses on the basis of the Catholic confession and the Catholic church. Just as from the beginning Hans Küng's efforts to make progress in ecumenical theology and the critical clarification of important questions of principle largely found recognition, so too his further investigations of the dialogue within religion about faith and morality, which deliberately started from the Council Declaration *Nostra Aetate*, have had a lasting influence. Since in any case Hans Küng's retirement has brought about a new situation, we request the church authorities, and especially the Bishop of Rottenburg-Stuttgart, Dr Walter Kasper, and the Roman Congregation of Faith to reassess the present situation. As a Catholic Faculty of Theology we call for the complete rehabilitation of Hans Küng as a Catholic theologian.[25]

However, in the end we can understand the conflicts over Küng's theology only when we see that for this Catholic theologian, catholicity is a 'still incomplete' project – for all the Christian churches. For the ideal of catholicity is something different from the ideology of 'Catholicism' or 'Protestantism': a self-righteous claim to the truth by one Christian church, at the expense of all the others, which stems from the petty-mindedness which draws dividing lines and excludes. All the churches still have to achieve this catholicity. It is rooted in loyalty to the gospel and has its 'signs' in extension over space, in the numerical quantity of its members, in its cultural and social variety, and in the great age of its 'marks', its signs – no more and no less.[26] So the motive force behind Küng's theology is not a cheap polemic against institutions or hierarchies but the concept of another catholicity in the interest of the ecumenicity of the church, with a precise theological foundation.

To achieve this catholicity of the church it was also necessary to rethink theologically the Vatican I dogmas relating to the pope (papal primacy and papal infallibility), because they had served to isolate the Latin Western Church of Rome from the other churches of Christianity and had put unnecessary hindrances in the way of the full unity of the churches. Küng's 'Inquiry' into this special Roman tradition therefore did not arise either from an 'anti-Roman feeling' or from a rationalistic and anti-dogmatic scepticism. In a concern for the ecumene it arose from the same centre of his theology: that the church of Jesus Christ will be maintained in the truth by the God who alone is infallible. Here the 'Inquiry' did not seek to give impetus to a democratic enthusiasm at the base (as though for Küng the church was only a movement and not also a structure; only an experience and not also a tradition; only subjectivity and not also subjection to a binding confession). Küng always supported the movement 'from below' within the church when it embodied characteristics of the New Testament form of the community. In terms of structural politics the 'Inquiry' into the infallibility and primacy of the pope ultimately aimed at another constitutional model of the Catholic church, which takes seriously the concerns of the Protestant and Anglican models of the church and at the same time tries to avoid their defects. In overcoming an unbiblical papalistic centralism deriving from the Middle Ages, the Catholic church is not concerned to imitate Geneva or Canterbury but to have its own concept of spiritual leadership, the power of which is controlled by conciliar and synodical structures – as checks and balances – and which thus can be accepted within both the church and the ecumene.

This definition of catholicity by a Catholic reform theology is a challenge to all the confessions that have grown up. It calls for a farewell to the Catholic illusion that the unity of the churches could be achieved by the return of the other churches to an unchanged Roman Catholic 'paternal home'. At the same time it calls for a farewell to a Protestant self-satisfaction which thinks that it does not need to reflect on the Catholic elements (in ministry and sacraments) which it has lost. Here a

Catholic reform theology is claiming its own right as what F. Herr has called a 'third force'.[27] It has to assert itself against a Protestant feeling of superiority which feeds on the conviction that the Catholic reform agenda has long been implemented in Protestantism and can most easily be settled by a conversion to Protestantism. But it also has to assert itself over against a Catholic traditionalism which tends to denounce the same agenda for reform with reference to the allegedly miserable state of modern Protestantism, so that everything can be left as it was. A Catholic reform theology in the spirit of Erasmus of Rotterdam and of Catholic humanism is more interested in the concerns of the other churches and modernity, without failing to recognize the dialectic of modern Protestantism and the Enlightenment. Learning from both, without succumbing to either, it fights for an ecumenical openness of Catholicism at a world level: allowing the validity of the other without losing its own substance and profile.

Dimension 4. An ecumenical reconciliation between the Christian churches

After all this, there need hardly be any long explanations of why from the same centre of his theology Hans Küng is concerned for a reconciliation between the separated Christian churches: with matter-of-factness, passion and perspicacity. And that he considers the continuation of the excommunication between the churches of the Reformation and the church of Rome at the end of the second millennium to be a scandal in church history. However, no one could see how far we would progress along the way of reconciliation in 1957, when Küng presented his study of the doctrine of justification and gained the highly personal approval of Karl Barth for the thesis that what had been identified as the specific feature of the Protestant Reformation over against the Catholic tradition, the doctrine of the justification of the sinner, need not – if rightly understood – separate the churches any longer . . .

But all at once a great deal else had changed, sparked off by the Second Vatican Council. All at once Catholic and Protestant theologians began working with one another, openly and without reservations. Karl Barth's conversations for the years 1959 to 1962, which have just been published, provide material here which is as instructive as it is amusing. In 1960 Karl Barth was in conversation with members of the Herrnhut community of brethren: 'There are voices in the Catholic world which claim that they can detect an agreement between my doctrine of justification and their own. This has happened, for instance, in Hans Küng's book. It is a very bold book. Directly under the nose of His Holiness Küng has ploughed through my *Church Dogmatics*. He must take the responsibility: I told him that he is Catholic and I am Protestant. But he is convinced that his view will win through in Catholicism. I asked him whether he would still say that if he were pope – he is still a young man. He thought he would. "We believe," he said, "that the gospel also has power there." There are Catholic theologians with whom I like to chat much better than with some Protestant theologians.'[28]

No, the times of Catholic anti-Protestantism and Protestant anti-Catholicism were over with these breakthroughs. Catholic and Protestant theologians began to discover things they had in common and to anticipate the ecumene in microcosm: in parishes, universities, schools, action groups of all kinds and not least in the course of the conciliar process for peace, justice and the preservation of creation. Such an anticipation of the ecumene was given expression in a way I shall never forget when after reading Küng's book *The Church*, the Protestant exegete Ernst Käsemann declared that the schism between him and Küng was now over. And even Karl Barth could remark to Küng: 'What a pity that you're a Catholic! Otherwise you could have become my successor!'[29]

So we can say without exaggeration that the overcoming of schism, not the realization of a uniform church but rather the abolition of the excommunication within Christianity at the local level, is one of the most powerful motive forces behind Küng's theology. The debate which he provoked about papal infallibilty also has its deepest motive here, in the awareness that there will be no reconciliation of the partial churches of Constantinople, Wittenberg, Geneva and Canterbury with the partial church of Rome unless previously the papal dogmas of the First Vatican Council have been rethought and re-received by the whole of the ecumene. Here the Second Vatican Council opened doors. For with its Decree on Ecumenism it has finally committed the Catholic Church to the cause of ecumenism. Now being a Catholic no longer means being anti-ecumenical. From the Catholic side, rather, after the texts of Vatican II it must be conceded that the limits of the church of Jesus Christ are not identical with the limits of the visible Catholic church. For the sake of the fullness of its own catholicity, the Catholic Church must be ecumenically open. So the catholicity of the church in the full sense will be truly realized only in communion with the previously separated Christian churches.

If it is realized, there will no longer be any confessionalism which thinks that it is in the right, but basic Christian attitudes which have grown up in history that can now complement one another. The constant reminder to the Christian that there is no other norm for living and dying than that of the gospel and that constant protest is in place should the gospel be betrayed is then 'Protestant'. And constant reflection on the universality of the church in space and time, on the establishment of the gospel in all cultures and nations, is 'Catholic'. In short, for Küng and others the vision already entertained by the great ecumenical figures Nathan Söderblom and Friedrich Heiler will become possible: a living form of 'evangelical catholicity', in which Christians attempt to be evangelical in a catholic way or catholic in an evangelical way.[30]

In theology, it takes the perspicacity of a Protestant theologian not only to discover this catholicity of Hans Küng's theology but also to express it publicly. Eberhard Jüngel has done this in exemplary fashion, and his text therefore deserves lengthy documentation:

> Catholic through and through – that is what Hans Küng has not only *remained* but *increasingly become*, not least in the controversy with his own Roman Catholic partial church: when he put the infallibility of the church's magisterium in question to argue all the more strongly that the church is maintained in truth by the God who alone is infallible; when with growing impatience he called not only on German bishops and cardinals but also on the pope himself

for an unhindered continuation of the intentions of the Second Vatican Council – aimed at openness not only to the other Christian churches but also to the 'modern world'. In so doing he was not afraid of sharp, indeed the sharpest criticism, from the institutionalized leadership of the church, but rather also included the Protestant church governments in his criticism, because today they do not do not even accuse Rome of what five hundred years earlier the Reformation had charged Rome with, etc., etc.

Yes, from the beginning Hans Küng has been, remained and increasingly become catholic through and through. He has been catholic in the original and real sense of the word, one who aims at *totality* and is thinking in terms of an identity, continuity and universality which is proving itself superior to all the confessional and cultural differences. Catholicity is always concerned with the whole.

Like every good theologian, Küng knows and insists that this universality has its centre in the gospel of Jesus Christ and only there, and therefore has its criterion of truth in everything that deserves to be called Christian, concentrated on the truth of the gospel. And so anyone who seriously attempts to be a Christian can and must be catholic in an evangelical way or evangelical in a catholic way. That is what Hans Küng teaches. He is right.

Hans Küng is obligated to this catholic truth concentrated on the gospel in his very own way. It gives his theological existence an unprecedented breadth, without ever causing it to lose its contours. It can probably be explained from his unprecedented will to accomplish things. It has turned the Roman German-

Theology in Freedom

ist into a penetrating ecumenist who wants to make the church, which is only too often preoccupied in talking to itself in a provincial way – though there is also so to speak a global provincialism which exports itself all over the world – capable of dialogue with the other Christian confessions; capable of dialogue with the world religions; capable of coming to an understanding which is no less difficult with cultures and civilizations that mistrust one another. And all this with a demand for practical consequences, which recently have come to include Küng's call for a minimal ethical consensus of all religions and world-views, on which a future global ethic can and should build.[31]

Dimension 5. A dialogical existence with the non-Christian religions

Indeed, the dialogue between the confessions and the dialogue between the religions, the internal ecumenism and the external ecumenism, are two sides of one and the same coin in Küng's work. This starts from the insight that Christian theology can no longer be responsible theology without a discussion with the world religions which compete with one another in their claim to the truth.

To survey the complex of problems here, Küng needed three phases of work. In the 1960s came the replacement of the traditional theology which held that the mass of unbaptized Christians were not damned with a theology of the universal will of God for salvation. A Christian theology of the religions came into being which, though still limited to the question of salvation, already shows a positive interest in the values of other religions.[32] In the 1970s for the first time the world religions were taken seriously as the constant horizon for the formation of Christian identity and the first attempts were made at a comparative account of religion: Jesus in the cross of co-ordinates of the founders of religion.[33] The 1980s saw the breakthrough to an understanding of the religions from within. Christians no longer theologize 'about' the world religions but speak in dialogue with the representatives of the religions.[34] The presupposition of this is respect for the self-understanding of those who are different, taking seriously other people's testimonies to faith, their spiritual and moral values, which in individual questions does not exclude a 'discernment of the spirits' in the light of the Christian understanding of faith. The concept of an inter-religious ecumenical theology is developed which is driven by a concern for the well-being of all religions, in the awareness that all religions are involved where in one of them there are violations of human rights and human dignity, or people abuse religion for purposes of power and authority . . . [35]

However, Hans Küng has also described the danger of being lost as a believing Christian in the oceans of the other world religions. As a Christian one can literally be submerged. One can sink, or want to remain in the supposedly safe haven of one's own faith because of an excess of anxiety. Here for Küng two things are important. First, the comparison between religions must be carried out truthfully and unsparingly: Christianity is not *a priori* superior to all other religions. But at the same time a comparison of religions can show that the centre of Christianity, the person and cause of Jesus Christ, need not fear any comparison. Comparisons can reinforce faith and need not destroy it. For comparisons between the great founders of religion also show the uniqueness of Jesus of Nazareth. They make possible a real choice, a real decision. None of this can be developed here, but it is expressed in a short poem by Dorothee Sölle, which reflects well the gist of Hans Küng's views on this question:

> Compare him quietly with other greats
> socrates
> rosa luxemburg
> gandhi
> he bears comparison
> with them all
> but it is better
> if you compare him
> with yourself.[36]

Here too the revolution in Hans Kung's generation of theologians is striking. Here is the abandonment of single-perspective ecclesiocentric thought and a consequent acceptance of a poly-perspectivistic multi-religious thought. In other words, here Christian theology is practised with a constant exchange between the internal and external perspectives: it is a matter of being resolute for what is Christian, but at the same time being prepared to incorporate in one's reflection the standpoint of those of other faiths. In other words, here is thinking in many perspectives, not as a lapse into relativism but as the achievement of a higher complexity of thought which attempts to do justice to a world that is becoming an increasingly complex network, even of religions.

The same centre of truth also makes itself felt in this dimension. The foundation of a theology of religions is the idea of the *Deus semper major*. If this is the starting point for Christians' thought, they will be capable of dealing with those of other faiths – in Karl Barth's sense – with full awareness and at the same time humbly and modestly. For if the incomprehensible, mysterious God is himself the truth, then even Christians cannot claim to understand him, the Incomprehensible; they cannot claim to have grasped him, the Unfathomable. For according to Paul even Christians know the truth only as in a 'mirror', in 'enigmatic and sketchy form', in fragments . . . And it follows from this for Küng that in its encounter with the other religions even Christianity has to understand itself as being on the way: *ecclesia peregrinans, homines viatores*. And as encounters are incalculable, so too the future of the religions is incalculable. Who knows what christology, qur'anology or buddhology will look like in the year 2096? According to Küng only one thing is certain:

At the end both of human life and the course of the world there will not be Buddhism or Hinduism, nor Islam and Judaism either. Indeed at the end there will not even be Christianity. At the end there will be no religion, but the one Inexpressible towards whom all religions are directed, and whom even Christians first only know fully, as they themselves are known, when the imperfect gives way to the perfect: *the* truth face to face. So at the end there will no longer be a Prophet or an Enlightened One, a Muhammad and a Buddha, causing separation between the religions. Indeed even Jesus the Christ, in whom Christians believe, will no longer be a factor of separation. But he to whom according to Paul all powers (including death) are then subjected "will subject himself" to God, so that God himself – or whatever he may be called in the East – is truly not only in all but *all in all* (I Cor. 15.28).[37]

The consequence

I have spoken of the centre and of five dimensions of Hans Küng's theology. To conclude, I want to speak of a personal consequence of the theology of freedom: boldness in public. Paul uses a word for this, *parrhesia*, which means openness in speaking which does not hide or conceal, stating one's views in public without hindrance. Courage means not being afraid, but it also means delight and trust; it means going one's way in joyful confidence.

It is all the more necessary to be joyful and not to be deterred, the more a Catholic theology of reform becomes aware of the terrifying time-lags with which it is confronted. By this I mean that since the end of the Council thirty years ago and the end of the German Synod in Würzburg twenty years ago energies have been wasted in the vague implementation of a reform agenda within the church repeated like a prayer wheel (from sexual morality to questions of ecumenism, the ministry and the ordination of women). There is probably no theologian committed to reform who has not felt surges of anger over how much strength has been wasted in debates about the inner structure of the church, strength which has been lost to grappling with the real challenges of the time. This strength should have been used grappling with a post-Christian society which is already in the majority – at least in the urban centres of Germany – and grappling with the world in which millions of people live, stamped by the work industry on the one hand and the entertainment industry on the other. Along with Hans Küng, all those who are committed to the reform of the church are fed up with a theological existence which gives us a twisted neck, because time and again the problems of the past force us to look behind us instead of keeping our gaze fixed forwards.

And like Küng, many of us are impatient with the demands that come from within the church, impatient not because of an arrogant feeling that we know better, but because of an often desperate bewilderment that we are still disputing over problems which we thought we had settled, both theologically and intellectually. The sharpness of many attitudes does not stem from a delight in polemic but from sorrow at what is still unresolved. Aggression against the demonic way in which tradition, patriarchalism, confessionalism and papal centralism arc idolizcd docs not arise out of an indifference to what is Catholic but out of a love for the cause of the church, which we would prefer to see in a better position. We would like to see a church related to its beginning and to the present, a church of brothers and sisters, a church which is ecumenically open and universal, truly catholic, in which catholicity is the power to affirm even the stranger, according to the saying of the apostle to the world: 'Test everything; hold fast to what is good' (I Thess. 5.21).

Here too a story keeps running round in my mind. It was my first seminar with Hans Küng, in the winter of 1969/70. He invited us students to his home – it must have been in February 1970. His manuscript *Infallible?*

was in a drawer and during the course of the evening Küng could not resist reading us a particular bit of the foreword. Catholic theologians hitherto had had to get the 'imprimatur', official permission to publish from the church, for all their books. What did Küng do? He wrote: 'No imprimatur will be sought for this book; not because it is not intended to be Catholic, but because – as we hope – it is Catholic without it.'[38] He himself laughed most at this brilliant coup. And this laughter is so typical of him: there is an echo here of the William Tell resistance of the Swiss Confederacy, a bit of the wicked delight of one who is fighting from below, that he has been able to cock a snook at the powerful; a bit of courage in the face of anxiety about the consequences that might threaten; a bit of hope that he would succeed in getting away from the apron strings to which Catholic theology was tied. Here is theology from a liberated and responsible freedom.

Laughter as an expression of resistance, of joy, of the overcoming of anxiety, of unquenchable hope – in short, militant humour: that is Küng's variant of the Pauline *parrhesia*. Here is laughter as a banishment of the spirits of resignation and cynicism – despite Sloterdijk's conceited *bon mot*.[39] Perhaps this is the most important thing that we, Hans Küng's pupils, owe to him: by indefatigable scholarly work on difficult questions of faith he has showed us possible solutions and so kept alive faith that the great cause of theology is worth every effort and all creativity – on the basis of scholarly thoroughness, imaginative fantasy and mental stamina. In the more than twenty years during which we have worked together, I have often seen Hans Küng exhausted or furious, worn out or angry, but I have never seen him without delight in a new intellectual adventure, without intellectual curiosity, without his militant humour. This is reflected yet again in a remark made by Erasmus of Rotterdam to Martin Luther, which Hans Küng has appropriated as the reason why he himself remains in the church: 'So I shall tolerate this church until I see a better one, and it is compelled to put up with me until I myself improve.'[40]

Farewell to Hans Küng

Tübingen, spring 1960. While the university, after years of expansion, was getting ready to welcome its ten-thousandth student, a man highly regarded by his colleagues for his learning and gentle nobility was sitting in the Dean's office of the Catholic Theology Faculty, writing to a young scholar who had just arrived at the Wilhelmsstift, and was about to occupy the Chair of Fundamental Theology.

The young scholar's name was Hans Küng. He was Swiss, and had seen something of the world between Lucerne and Rome, Paris and Münster (where, under the aegis of Herman Volk, he had worked as an academic assistant), weatherproof and polyglot.

The letter, dated May, from Professor Joseph Möller to Dr Hans Küng in the Wilhelmsstift, began:

> Dear Colleague,
> A warm welcome to Tübingen! Unfortunately I have another engagement from ten o'clock onwards, so may I perhaps ask you, if you are not too tired, to look in at the Dean's office just after 9 (New Aula, Second Floor, Room 38).
> Warmest good wishes,
> Joseph Möller,
> Dean.

Here is a letter from a time long past. In those days, unlike today on the computer, one did not get straight to the point. First of all there is a greeting; then the letter does not say 'I expect you', but 'May I perhaps ask you', and this 'may' and 'perhaps' are further qualified by an 'if you are not too tired', as though a time-lag had to be taken into account after a journey from Münster to Tübingen. And that for someone who had been brought up in the harsh school of the Gregoriana in Rome and had been accustomed from his youth to subject himself to the rule of exercises from the crack of dawn: the short nights were followed by long hours of meditation, reading, writing and disputation – in Latin, of course. Naturally Joseph Möller knew all this, but like many scholars of his stamp, he had grown up in an age in which there was still respect for the maxims of Immanuel Kant. Kant, though close to death, rose from his chair to welcome the Rector, who compelled him to sit down: 'I have not yet forgotten a sense of humanity.' So Joseph Möller – those were the days – qualified his request by an 'if' and a 'perhaps', and asked the new professor to look in on passing instead of, as has meanwhile become the custom, offering him a specific appointment.

Now we may presume that the worthy gentleman from Switzerland, youthful and with a shock of wavy hair, will certainly have knocked at the door on the second floor of the New Aula ahead of time, and will have been welcomed by a scholar – Möller seemed a little other-worldly; he needed a special kind of air to protect his thoughts – for whom it was not too much trouble to help newcomers look for accommodation and to seek a home appropriate for modest, celibate circumstances. As a letter of 24 May 1960 puts it:

Herr Director Herre is prepared to put a room at your disposal in the Wilhelmsstift until another solution presents itself . . . It is a guest room, and therefore not a small study. [In other words, not inappropriate for the worthy gentleman and *Ordinarius* Professor elect.] Another possibility which might certainly be considered would be two rooms, but these are on the edge of the town. However, these rooms would first have to be got ready, and in addition you would have to have a cleaning woman, since the old lady who might possibly rent these rooms is already more than seventy years old. I have discovered another possibility in today's paper and am enclosing the advertisement (*Schwäbisches Tagblatt*, Tübingen).

In fact Hans Küng was welcomed in a way which was not only friendly but even paternal, before spending seventy-two semesters in that small town to whose greatness he was to contribute so much during the coming decades all over the world, between the Neckar, the Tiber and the Hudson.

No, he will not have regretted the fact that on 16 May 1960, after a short introduction and, we may presume, the warmest greetings on both sides, he had told the Dean: 'I would like to take this opportunity to express my most sincere thanks once again to you and all the gentlemen of the faculty (at that time there were no women) for the great honour that you are doing me. I look forward very much to my teaching work at your university.' (Hans Küng had written 'university', not 'faculty', a distinction which was once again to prove significant.)

To begin with, everything was fine. True, some clouds

were already gathering, especially in Rome. The manuscript of *The Council and Reunion* was arousing suspicion, and professors and cardinals of the Curia were showing signs of anxiety. However, on the other side there was a man like Cardinal König, who made a plea for an *imprimatur* which was as personal as it was emphatic – and as for the local situation, it was not only friendly, but enthusiastic. 'I am delighted,' Dean Möller told him, 'that you are coming to us and (once again) offer you a warm welcome . . . I hope that you will like it here and ask you to give my warmest good wishes to my colleague Herr Volk.' (It should be noted in passing that this request was not without a touch of piquancy: since he had come to know about *The Council and Reunion*, Volk was following Hans Küng's journalism with the utmost scepticism: here, it seemed to him, a man was going his own way.) 'And I wish you,' the letter which made Hans Küng one of us ended, 'much joy in your lecturing in Tübingen.' There has been plenty of that, thank God, down to the present day, despite all the turbulence.

At any rate, the harmony in 1960 was complete. The solution which had been found – a man who had not written a habilitation thesis but who promised much as successor to Heinrich Fries – soon proved ideal. And how long a road it had been, at the end of the 1950s, before this solution had finally been reached!

First of all there was the story which I have reconstructed from the faculty archives (thanks to Dean Niehr and the secretary, Frau Härle), which deserves to be retold and, since it takes place at a high level, between Stuttgart and Rome, makes extremely exciting reading. Initially everything went along the familiar lines.

Bernhard Welte from Freiburg was called by common consent, but who would choose to leave a city characterized by casual south German Catholicity and moreover famed for its admirable gastronomy, to move to our meagre Protestant 'Neckar-Tübingen', a *village* (as David Friedrich Strauss and Friedrich Theodor Vischer called it with decided abhorrence) in which there have certainly been many geniuses between Kepler and Hegel, but also legions of rabid pietistic brothers and sisters, including theologians on whom it was asserted that the Holy Spirit did not descend in the form of a dove but in that of a raven?

So Bernhard Welte entertained the matter only briefly. He indicated that it was pleasant to be called to a professorial chair which – who knows? – was preferable to all others because it offered the possibility (that Hans Küng was later to exploit excessively) 'of developing an independent programme in collegial sympathy with neighbouring disciplines', but then he declined. As expected, the ambience was the crucial factor: to give up the Vosges and the Black Forest for the Swabian Alps; the cathedral for the Stiftskirche – the question was already settled!

So the time came when the authorities in Stuttgart began to get restless: the gentlemen put in second and third place, who had spent their days, worthily and in tranquillity, in Paderborn and Dilligen (and, it was to be feared, expected to end them there), hardly aroused any enthusiasm.

So what was to be done? Look round again among the local young professors who were very promising? But the faculty had already done this. Gottlieb Söhngen in Munich had long since cast his vote: Joseph Ratzinger,

Professor of Dogmatics in Freising – who else? ('With his extraordinary gifts and his amazing diligence Ratzinger has a significant future ahead of him.') Unfortunately, however, in Bavaria, despite the slogan *extra Bavariam nulla vita*, which – who knows? – is perhaps current even today, this man had decided for Bonn, though of course later he came to Tübingen.

The years when Hans Küng and Joseph Ratzinger worked together with us were years of friendship: the editor of the university journal *Attempto*, who in 1968 was Walter Jens, with real enjoyment put articles on 'Infallible Magisterium?' (by Hans Küng) and 'Tendencies in Catholic Theology' (by Joseph Ratzinger) side by side, followed by articles from Jürgen Moltmann ('God and Resurrection') and Hermann Diem ('The Public Task and the Public Claim of the Church'). That was truly an attractive issue!

Was the editor aware of the conjuring trick he had pulled off at that time? I think so. The preface to the issue, dated December 1968, speaks for itself:

Here is a theological issue, topical and profound. That is how it was planned, and the result has far exceeded all dreams. We were certain of the articles by Diem and Moltmann, but from where were we to get parallel representation from the other faculty, which would be just as good? Hans Küng referred to a book that was in the press – and an essay from that could be given an introduction for *Attempto*; Joseph Ratzinger intimated that he could provide something more fundamental – but a dose of 'flu jeopardized the enterprise. And then, this stroke of luck. There, after all, was the fundamental article by Ratzinger, a basis for ongoing reflections, and alongside it, rising boldly into the air, a rocket fired from the Marches of Switzerland and now circling over Tübingen . . . and prompting the editor to ask: 'If the pope does not read *Attempto* – how could we send him a copy of our journal?' Our thanks to the theologians . . . editors are lucky to have such good fortune once in ten years.

Küng and Ratzinger, for a short time united in our city by the Neckar, each in his own way called our century to account.

That, unfortunately, is the end of the excursus (spinning out the vision of a discordant concord, it could easily have gone on longer). Once again, for a moment, we must return to the pre-Küng era at the end of the 1950s, after the end of the hopes for Bernhard Welte. In Stuttgart – thank God – people began to bang their fists on the table. Was a giant like Heinrich Fries and his heritage in Pader-Dillingen to be forgotten? Unthinkable. As you were! 'Put in your first team' was the motto: Hans Urs von Balthasar and no one else. Certainly there were plenty of reservations; after all, Balthasar, after being called to a chair of dogmatics, had once again come to grief by being refused a *nihil obstat*. But this time – as Bishop Leiprecht of Rottenberg knew from a reliable source – Rome would give its consent. There could be no objections to his occupying the chair for fundamental theology.

And lo and behold, the wires began to hum; the inner wheels began turning: Pater Roberto Leiber, Pope Pius XII's private secretary, was drawn into the Stuttgart plans; indeed Gebhard Müller, Prime Minister and later President of the Federal Constitutional Court, indicated an approach to John XXIII. And all this – at this point I have to correct myself – even before Welte had actually said no. Balthasar was the one. What about that? Of course no one wanted to put pressure on the Faculty, since the decision was theirs. But, how would it be if first of all the bishop made soundings, quite unofficially, among friends?

Now Lieprecht wrote – and so too did Balthasar, but not as hoped for. Certainly he expressed to the bishop his 'most humble and reverential thanks for all the – unpleasant! – things that he has done for me and for the burdens imposed on him. But attractive though it is, this chair does not fit in with all my plans for my life.'

Helvetia locuta causa finita: what was left for the supreme pastor of Rottenberg than – as happened in January 1959 – to communicate Balthasar's categorical and clear no to the faculty: indicated privately, but now made official by the bishop's letter?

Indeed this was an exciting drama! The chair for fundamental theology at a German university the centre of efforts at the highest level – and with what actors! What scenes! What illustrious names, which have stamped the theology of our time: Ratzinger, Balthasar, and finally Küng!

Yes, Hans Küng. When the list of potential professors seemed to fade away to nothing (meanwhile even Dilligen had shown Tübingen the cold shoulder), the Ministry decided upon a liberating stroke. It was even prepared to call a theologian who had not passed the habilitation examination if, in scholarship and character(!), he seemed suitable to occupy the chair of fundamental theology.

The faculty and the senate breathed again. An extension to the list – that was the solution, certainly not a makeshift solution but an ideal one. Hans Küng, living in Münster in Westphalia, Frauenstrasse 5–6, was proposed by the faculty in a *laudatio* the tenor of which makes today's readers ask: 'Why not immediately?' 'Why all these toings and froings?' As the senate orator Ernst Zinn put it:

> Everything known about Küng's development and personality suggests that the teaching experience which he so far lacks will rapidly be acquired in practice. Since his work thus far indicates such a strong interest in philosophy and ecumenics and controversial theology, his appointment would first of all take care of these two important areas for which the chair is responsible. But it is to be expected that the youthful energy he has shown so far in tackling central problems, and which makes Küng's arrival so promising, will in the future also be proved in the historical sphere, or in the sphere of fundamental theology in the narrower sense.

So the way was free, and Hans Küng could set to work in the autumn of 1960, surrounded by the goodwill of his colleagues, and soon given lively acclaim from among the ranks of the students. There were the verve, the élan and the broad perspectives opened up by a young, urbane, multilingual man who was acquainted with the world from top to toe, a Swiss citizen and cosmopolitan whose seminars were so solid that he was taken for a . . . but let us read what Küng's colleague and friend Herbert Haag (he is Küng's fellow-countryman in disposition and career – Lucerne, Paris and Tübingen! Practical ministry and industrious learning!) wrote in

1963 to a doctor named Fischer seeking information: 'We can tell you that Professsor Dr Hans Küng is not a Jesuit father but a priest of the diocese of Basel.'

Yes, Hans Küng was also a pastor, especially in his first years at Tübingen, when he loved to hold seminars on problems of ecclesiology – as this is manifested in Barth's *Church Dogmatics*, in the encyclical *Mystici Corporis* or in Calvin's *Institutes*. No wonder, from this perspective, that in a short time relations between Tübingen and Rottenberg became almost warm. In January 1962 the newly-called fundamental theologian – living at Gartenstrasse 103, Tübingen – asked the Ministry of Education to accede to Bishop Leiprecht's request to be accompanied by his adviser Hans Küng to Rome for the great council which was beginning on 11 October. 'I believe that this request must be met because of the importance of the church event, especially as in this way the good relations between the local bishop and the faculty will be demonstrated.'

Asked for and already approved – and more than once. Bishop Carl Joseph Leiprecht was also accompanied by his trusty *peritus* to the second session of the Council. The lectures could not begin until December – but what did that matter? A substitute was soon found, a man who knew his craft: 'At the suggestion of Professor Küng, until his return from Rome, Assistant Dr Walter Kasper will take over the lectures.' ('The Representative' in a Swabian setting: from today's perspective truly a separate configuration.)

But now came harder days, and not only the vexations experienced by Tübingen's brightest minds at all times: Vischer and Strauss for example, not to mention Romano Guardini, whom Carlo Schmid after the Second

World War would so gladly have bound firmly to Tübingen for all time. However, he did not know his Pappenheimer well: the wishes of the state government were 'wishes, not orders with which the Faculty has to comply', especially as Professor X on the basis of inquiries made among experts 'would regard Guardini's achievements more as noble edification than as scholarship'.

Tübingen's painful episodes over the centuries: the harrassment of free spirits who had to swear on the Formula of Concord of Protestant orthodoxy; old-fashioned pedantry in the name of supposed orthodoxy, the inhibiting of scholarly and private rebelliousness! There were times when the cry 'To Heidelberg' sounded almost as seductive in Tübingen as the melody of longing in Chekov's three sisters, 'To Moscow, To Moscow!'

Nevertheless, in the history of Tübingen, the *alma mater*, there had never been such dossiers as the Roman one which bears the inventory number 399/57i, a dossier with bulky files which imperceptibly turned the scholar Hans Küng into Kafka's land surveyor Josef K: a liberal man of God yesterday, still surrounded by the approving applause of his superiors, who suddenly found himself faced with an inquisition made up of warders and stewards, senior and junior officials, messengers and scribes, Latinists and sub-Latinists, custodians of the magisterium, representatives of the custodians and representatives of the representatives, all of whom commanded a highly specialized vocabulary ('report' was understood as 'colloquium', 'receipt of an order' as 'conversation') and, all things considered, used a language in their statements compared with which paragraphs from law books read as real poetry.

In the statement issued by the Congregation of Faith on 5 July 1973, we read:

Jesus Christ willed that the magisterium of the Supreme Pastors, to whom he has entrusted his mission to preach the gospel to all his people and to all the human family, has been endowed with the corresponding charism of infallibility in respect of questions of faith and morals. As such a charism cannot be derived from new revelations which the successors to Peter and the episcopal office could enjoy, these are not relieved of the need, with appropriate means, to investigate the treasury of the divine revelation in the holy books in which the truth caused by God to be written down for our salvation is taught without falsification . . . In the exercise of their office they have the help of the Holy Spirit. His support is most effective when they instruct the people of God by preaching a doctrine on the basis of the promises of Christ to Peter and all the other apostles which is necessarily free from error.

An objection, Your Honours, simply on linguistic grounds. An objection from an individual, the surveyor of the biblical land, Hans K, in the name of Jesus Christ: that Christ who, according to Küng in a convincing presentation of his view – once accepted by the Reformation, now ecumenical – never founded a church. As for the magisterium of the Supreme Pastor, after a long silence (which Dostoevsky once described), having had to have this term translated into Aramaic and then, having heard in amazement about the process of communication which evidently existed between heaven and

Rome – infallibly guaranteed – in solitude, as in the last sentence of the story of the Grand Inquisitor, 'the prisoner departs'.

However, the magisterium would have taken little notice of this gesture, which is the quintessence of Dostoevsky's tract, just as so far it has never seriously considered Hans Küng's inquiries based on scripture. 'If the popes in their Acts,' runs the central thesis of the encyclical *Humani generis*, for which Pius XII was responsible, 'adopt a position on a previously disputed question, then it is clear to all (*omnibus patet*), according to the intention and will of these same popes, that this question can no longer be regarded as an object of free discussion among theologians (*liberae inter theologos disceptationis*).'

When I read such statements, I think that it is truly time to subject the papal encyclicals of the last century, along with their authoritative statements which dispense with the exegesis of experts – above all New Testament scholars! – and which with the pontificate of the present pope amount to a mystagogy which is excessively degenerate, to precise analysis by inter-disciplinary symposia of theologians, linguists and literary critics, of course with Hans Küng as symposiarch.

A congress of international moral theologians stated on 12 November 1988 that the doctrine of the encyclical *Humanae vitae* was not just a doctrine devised by human beings but rather was 'inscribed by the divine creator's hand on the nature of the human person and endorsed by him in revelation'. ('So to subject it to discussion means refusing God himself the obedience of our understanding. It means that we prefer the light of our reason to the light of the divine wisdom.') To put it without fanaticism, this assertion, which amounts to the thesis that nine-tenths of humankind have failed to obey God, thanks to their rationally based practices in sexual matters, and have put God's holiness in question, calls for a refutation based on linguistic criticism and theology (what are we to understand by a 'writing creator's hand'?), taking account of the declaration *Pastor Aeternus* which, as the climax of the First Vatican Council, puts the pope in chains. And, as Hans Küng has emphasized time and again with the help of careful and humane consideration of the souls of the Holy Fathers, to free him from these chains would mean breaking with the whole tradition. In so far as it contradicted the previous central theses, even the most rational 'no' would contain the concession that the Holy Spirit had erred – and with it the magisterium.

It is gripping to read how intensively Hans Küng in particular, taking as an example the Montini pope, whom his predecessor, John XXIII, apostrophized as Hamlet ('Amleto'), the hesitating and scrupulous intellectual on Peter's throne, has analysed the inexorability predetermined by the First Vatican Council which even the most liberal pope cannot evade – not to mention the doctrinaire popes, compared with whose declarations Leo X's bull *Exsurge Domine*, in which Martin Luther's errors are enumerated (there are forty-one of them, including the thesis, 'That heretics are to be burned is against the will of the Spirit') seems almost humane. At any rate, it is stamped by a skill in colourful variation: 'We condemn, disapprove of or reject all and several of the aforementioned articles or errors as being utterly . . . heretical or offensive or false or injurious to pious ears or leading simple spirits astray and opposed to the

Catholic truth.' *Piarum aurium offensivos vel simplici-um mentium seductivos*: this richly varied diction is balm compared with the imperious monotony and the dull recapitulation of the one and only pattern, 'God has commanded that . . . ', of contemporary decisions.

And here – a thesis which Hans Küng has been concerned to put into practice for decades – it is possible to speak of God not just in insipid administrative language with its sinister actuarial Latin and schematically repeated formulae and sentences. A few sentences from Augustine's *Confessions* are enough to make us forget the administrative jargon of Denziger scholasticism: 'You have called, cried, broken the spell of my dumbness, have thundered, lightened and dispelled my blindness. I have breathed your fragrance and I sigh for you. I have tasted you and now I hunger and thirst. You have touched me and I am on fire with longing for your peace.'

I shall never forget the days in the summer of 1945, a few weeks after the liberation of our land from National Socialism, when I read the tenth book of Augustine's *Confessions* in my parents' home in Hamburg with Ernst Zinn, who was later to be the senate reporter in matters relating to Küng. We noted the well laid out structure with its parallelisms and antitheses, rhythm and clausulae, the sum of which is a mystery of unparalleled rhetorical prose, calculated in every detail, even down to the refinement of the changes of colons and tenses, yet nevertheless enthusiastic: *vocasti et clamasti et rupisti surditatem meam, corucasti, splenduisti et fugisti caecitatem meam, fragrasti et duxi spiritum et anhelo tibi, gustavi et esurio et sitio, tetigisti me et exarsi, in pacem tuam.*

That is high solemnity, deeply moving eloquence, and not formulaic Latin from registries and offices. Hans Küng can appreciate this splendour of the rhetorical art, though of course it does not prevent him from always being a little suspicious of it. He now prefers Sallust to Cicero and Augustine – of course using John XXIII's ruler.

A ruler? What does that mean? The Roman *peritus* from the friendly days used to enjoy telling how the pope from Bergamo, when documents were set in front of him, would put his ruler by the margin and say: 'This sentence is more than seven centimetres long. Make it two. You will see that your thesis becomes sharper.'

Here was advice from Rome – and not the only advice – which has been followed in Tübingen. Hans Küng likes brevity: main clause after main clause, a prose structure which is convincing but only rarely makes the pulse beat faster. He prefers to leave the art of moving the audience, a genuine example of the orator's craft, to the poets, whose showmanship he admires – but only in moderation. Histrionic writers need to make their metaphors flash out; fundamental theologians can dispense with this. Their prose gives splendour by its precision – artistically varied and never becoming a formula.

When Hans Küng begins to teach, he does not disavow the scholastic who has learned to argue in Cartesian riding boots any more than the catechete, who in his *operationes spirituales* prefers to argue from the negative after the pattern: 'Is A perhaps right? No. Then perhaps B? Hardly (at best). Then C? Again wrong.' Only after negatively modest attempts at a solution does the only right answer follow, well considered and clearer than day: 'Jesus is neither . . . nor, is not any of this but rather

. . . is thus in truth', and now the voice is raised a little; for a moment it slips into the *genus movendi* without leaving out of account the third artifice available to any speaker of distinction, the *genus delectandi* – a way of speaking more subordinated to ethos than to solemnity.

So for Hans Küng teaching is first of all vivid instruction, strict, convincing (never over-persuasive) and occasionally a bit daring – above all when the master pupil of the Gregorian begins his lectures with the words: 'I shall divide my investigation into eleven points.' This is to make the audience, in accordance with an old precept for orators, at the same time attentive (*attentus*), ready to learn (*docilis*) and benevolent (*benevolus*) – and he achieves this aim best, as far as attentiveness and readiness to learn are concerned, with his announcements of how the material is arranged, lecture by lecture: one knows where one is and never loses the thread. Of course if the sections get too long, good will can sometimes ebb away: 'My God, he's only at point four, there are seven more to go and the clock is already at five past nine. How will it end?' These are the moments in which thanks to excessive benevolence, some hearers begin to reflect on the famous remark by the critic which runs: 'Yesterday evening at the premiere, when I looked at the clock at quarter past ten, I noticed that it was only quarter past nine.'

But enough! Hans Küng never completely lets go of the reins, and not just because every Monday morning he succeeds in including his audience as partners in his figures of thought. These are not hammered home nor pronounced in a magisterial way, nor with a cumulative 'thus and not otherwise' is the anti-papistical truth proclaimed, but in an act of pure thought it is cheerfully precogitated, always with a concern to make it comprehensible, while nevertheless always remembering the oratorical rule that says that it is the task of the speaker to strike a balance between the level of the public's intelligence and the difficulty of the subject-matter to be communicated, something that is not achieved by the beginner, but only by the master.

Hans Küng, an advocate of skilful speech – am I describing a friend by my own standards and utilizing theology with a hasty recourse to rhetoric? I think not. The man who, God willing, will also say of himself as an Emeritus *numquam minus sum otiosus quam si otiosus sum* (I am never less idle than when I am idle) is not least a master of the royal art of conversation. He finds monologues, among friends, wearisome; he would much rather learn something new than constantly be lecturing himself. (A conversationalist like Fontane thought in precisely the same way: the great conversationalists are fond of listening, to the disappointment of those who visit them. Goethe remained silent or got lost in trivia, sometimes for so long that it became painful, and Thomas Mann imitated him. He got bored if people quoted him.)

'May silence also be rated as highly among Christians as keeping secrets within the soul and a renunciation of cheerfulness and joyful laughter': such rules for spiritual behaviour formulated by Ambrose at the end of the fourth century do not worry Hans Küng. The monks may keep silent and the pulpit orators may swagger, the fathers of the confessional may give commands and the Supreme Pastors proclaim unassailable truths: *he* loves dialogue, talk between equals, friendly conversation and cheerful, light parlando. The culture of conversation shapes the scenery on the Waldhäusen heights, conversation in Platonic or Ciceronian syle: there has to be a touch of Florence, Cosimo and Lorenzo in a circle of friends, and of course of Paris, the Latin Quarter, in whose cafés Madame and Monsieur, Sartre and Simone de Beauvoir, joined the students in the evening.

It is a social life on the hill, from the morning team conversation to the evening with guests. Marianne Saur and Hans Küng are friends of the *comitas Helvetica et Suevica*, under whose spell profundity counts for little and friendly conversation, free from Habermas-like domination, for a great deal. Everyday companionship in conversation and meals – Eleonore Henn and Sybille Abt always there – have taken the place of monologizing ruminations in the cell; Luther in Tübingen has done away with a Spanish-Roman Ignatius. 'Indeed a dumb person is to be counted as a half-dead person compared with someone who speaks', we read in the 'Preface to the Psalter', and, 'there is no more powerful and noble work among human beings than to speak. Since human beings are most different from others by virtue of their speech, more than through their form.'

Luther as a domestic god in the Küng household? And not rather Erasmus, the friend of peace, whom in his *opera omnia* the fundamental theologian and ecumenist so likes to hold up as the true, indeed real, reformer and advocate of the third way? No, perhaps not, I thought when, in preparing this farewell speech, on the prompting of Guido Kisch I came upon anti-Jewish remarks in the letter of the humanist which even bear comparison with Luther's rabid hostility to everything Hebrew: 'This rabble will first flood Germany and then the rest of the earth.' 'There is nothing more hostile and dangerous to Christ's teaching than this plague.' 'In Italy there are many Jews and in Spain hardly any Christians. I fear that in these circumstances that plague once already suppressed will be able to rear its head again. And the Christian church should not attach so much value to the Old Testament.'

Those are statements which, if I am correct, have never been quoted by Hans Küng – statements which he perhaps really does not know (so that on saying farewell he can delight in Solon's dictum, 'I will become older and also learn indefatigably'); statements which must trouble him, for if anyone has worked out the Jewish element in Christianity, concentrated in the Jew Jesus, whose descendants have been murdered by the million, it is Hans Küng – consistently renouncing a tradition which even in the darkest times German Christians of a Protestant stamp did not put in question any more than did Catholic Supreme Pastors. As late as 1941, when the deportations had long since begun, Conrad Gröber, Archbishop of Freiburg, informed the faithful in his diocese that the death of Jesus was due to the 'incessant agitation of the Pharisees and the scribes, and the crowd which was so easy to influence': Jews as the arch-enemies and deadly foes of Christ! Jews with their 'lust to rule the world'! Jews, the adversaries of the Lord 'for ever and ever'. 'Over Jerusalem,' remarked Archbishop Conrad Gröber, 'rings out the mad but truthful curse of the Jews upon themselves, "His blood be on us and on our children." The curse has fulfilled itself in a frightful way. Right down to the present day.'

Written in Germany, to please a regime which sought to exterminate everything that – however remotely – recalled the heritage of the Jew Jesus, that recalled him,

Paul, or Peter, the embodiment of an immensely sympathetic fallible human being. Peter, a clown (whose heirs, as Heinrich Böll emphasizes, come among other places from Bergamo), a fisherman who got whatever he did wrong; Peter, the *miles gloriosus*, as Hans Blumenberg has described him in his treatise on the 'St Matthew Passion' – Peter the failure, Peter the Jew. I would like once again in liberal arts to have a conversation with Hans Küng about that first pope whose essence, as a harlequin from the house of Israel, has never been understood by his church, despite all the homage paid to him. The way in which he constantly got there too late, his boasting and the false estimations of the situation, all in all this nevertheless make him deeply lovable – at least more loveable than Paul.

Here, though, Hans Küng would emphatically object: 'This poetic licence is going too far.' The intellectual who, with a far superior mind, resists Peter to the face is beyond compare for him – sharply sketched and as unique as all the figures are in Küng's giant work: precisely fixed and exactly kept at the specific historical moment. Here nothing is spared and there are no friendly generalizations; by virtue of the evidence, the precise narrative art of bringing situations to life, which makes us witnesses of the times of triumph and even more the times of torment, martyrdom and misery, readers see before their eyes the cross on which the Jew was hung – a tortured man begging for mercy in his last solitude, one who has been abandoned; one who, unlike the supposedly infallible popes, has erred: 'You will experience the apocalypse before your death.'

To shed light on Christ in his sign-setting uniqueness, mirrored in the testimony of reliable women and men around him: a Catholic has set out on this task in dialogue with Ferdinand Christian Baur or Ernst Käsemann in Tübingen, an ecumenist who, first and last, is concerned with that religion of Christ which, according to Lessing, may in no way be identified with Christian religion: as little – we add, with an eye to Kierkegaard – as the politically sanctioned Christendom which became fossilized in dogma is to be mentioned in the same breath as a Christianity which sees itself stamped with the living spirit, the charism of the first hours.

The longer I steeped myself in Hans Küng's writings over the last months and weeks, the clearer it became to me that here questions have been raised which, instead of finding a speedy answer, in turn raise constantly new questions, in the sense of Kafka's axiom: 'Under your rising feet the steps grow upwards' – questions and problems to spell out which is the concern of that man who all his life has remained an advocate of the right cause because it is the only humane cause, the cause of the weary and insulted, the weak and disadvantaged, the cause of the excluded. It is the cause of those who have been tortured body and soul by the powers of the church, rebelling against its Lord's command for reconciliation, the 'witches' and 'heretics' (in the literal and metaphorical sense); the cause of all those in the darkness, especially including women, whom a man in Rome as late as 1988, in the apostolic brief *Mulieris dignitatem*, banished with the statement: 'If Christ called only men as his apostles, he behaved in a completely free way and had a right to do so.'

Truly, it is time – as Hans Küng shows in such a situation – for the church finally to practise brotherhood and sisterhood, in other words those equal rights among all human beings the claim for which enables it to be the partner of the other world religions: perhaps even to be in a position to carry the torch for them along the lines of Kant's thesis of the emancipation of philosophy from the demon of a fossilized theology.

'All are invited and no one is excluded' must be the central thesis of religions guaranteeing humanity, if one joins Hans Küng in looking at Paragraph 34 of the 1793 Constitution of the French Revolution, which has still not been put into practice today: 'The whole of society is oppressed if even one of its members is oppressed. Every individual member is oppressed if the whole of society is oppressed.'

Two statements – addressed to a world in which human rights should be observed and to a truly democratic church; two statements which became significant in Tübingen almost half a century ago, in 1948, when Karl Barth's writing 'Christian Community and Civil Community' was being passionately discussed in student Christian groups, a pamphlet in which we read – in anticipation of Hans Küng's central thesis:

> In the Christian community, in discipleship of Christ . . . there is no rule, but service. So as a civic community, too, it can only regard any rule which as such is not service as a state of sickness, and never as a normal state . . . Bismarck, not to mention Hitler, was therefore not a model statesman (despite the book of Bible readings on his bedside table!), because he basically wanted to build the state from above downwards; because he wanted to build his work on 'power in itself'.

Once again, these are statements like those later

formulated by Hans Küng. Barth's thesis that only with a radical direction of the gaze from above downwards, from the heavens into the dust where those victims suffer who must no longer be victims, would gain humanity and dignity for the world – certainly not as an equivalent but surely as a parable for the kingdom of God. Barth's thesis could serve as a motto and leitmotiv for *On Being a Christian* and for *Global Responsibility* in so far as Küng is a man who in the course of his life has become increasingly political. How much so is shown in an apparently marginal document which in truth is of deep significance for the whole of his work, his interpretation of Wagner's *Parsifal* as a drama at the end of which, in his view, the brutal world of monks and men is superseded by love, compassion and responsible activity directed towards the other: the *praxis pietatis* in the style of Lessing's *Nathan*.

'If God will and we are alive,' as our grandparents used to say, I hope that Hans Küng will find time, after completing his book on Islam, to commemorate an unforgettable co-operation between the two of us in Tübingen liberal arts by once again turning to art, to music, literature and painting. I hope he will be active in a sphere which – thank God – as a whole knows no rigid paradigm shift but, governed by the law of uncontemporaneity, recalls and anticipates the present while transcending it, reveres mnemosyne and depicts a concrete utopia in parable and image.

Dear friend, no reference to postmodernity is needed here; here the Enlightenment is to be understood as an incomplete project which, according to Jurgen Mittelstrass, cannot be identified, as Horkheimer and Adorno would have it, with 'self-development in purposive rationality and strategies of optimization' – in other words an enlightenment that hinders enlightenment. Anyone who considers all that has not been achieved from that great age of emancipation which provides slogans to all fundamentalisms should, rather, reflect that Kant was very well aware why he distinguished between reason, which for him was a unity of *raison* and *coeur*, and understanding, and that in his *Education of the Human Race* Lessing specifically vindicated religion as an element of progress: not a hindrance but a motive force on the way to the universal liberation of human beings at a time when revelation and reason, divine providence and human co-operation, were combined in the realization of a great building plan.

In an exemplary scene which has not been surpassed, the Jew Nathan demonstrates what enlightenment is, in conversation with the monks – after the holocaust to which he has to surrender his seven sons, and after the rescue of one person, the Christian girl Recha: 'Nathan, Nathan,' cry the monks, 'You are a Christian! There never was a better one!' To which Nathan retorts: 'Good for us, for what makes me a Christian for you, makes you Jews for me. But let us no longer simply avoid one another. Here action is needed.'

This is what I call a foretaste of *Global Responsibility* in the eighteenth century – overcoming the scholasticism of the paradigms. Literature, not to mention music – and this is a firm reminder to Hans Küng – is not fixed on a paradigmatic mainstream. Rather, it anticipates what often enough only becomes reality centuries later; it is ahead of its time and yet at the same time sees to it that what has apparently been superseded never passes away. So it cannot be grasped by a concept like post-

modernity, simply because before it, in happy moments
– though these are all too rare – all 'pre's and 'post's
become insignificant.

You will see that I do not want the spheres of the
laudandus and his *laudator* to coincide too closely. In
the future we shall also have to go on learning from each
other, on the frontiers of theology and literature – not
forgetting homiletic in the wider sense, whose rules
Hans Küng – as one can read in 'Guidelines for a
Contemporary Theology' – has analysed as a discipline
with a binding quality, engaged in scholarly interdisci-
plinarity, dialogical exchange and ecumenical reflection,
and with a relationship to praxis. Moreover – if we
survey his audiences scattered over the continents – it
is highly effective: stamped by charisma, learning and
narrative wit, in the style of the Enlightenment.

Teaching students and non-students alike, Hans Küng
has achieved a masterpiece that even Schiller would
have noisily applauded – and he, God knows, had more
perfect control of the art of speech that goes to the heart
than any other, except of course Luther and Lessing –
had he met Hans Küng in the lecture hall on a Monday
evening. We read in a letter of 12 August 1787 to
Gottfried Körner,

> I heard Herder preach. The text was the unjust steward,
> with which he grappled with much understanding and
> subtlety. The whole sermon was like a discourse that
> a man carries on alone, extremely popular in style, of
> course, less a speech than a rational conversation. A
> principle applied from applied philosophy: teach what
> one could just as well have expected in a mosque as in
> a Christian church . . . He feels that he is a superior

intellect, surrounded by utterly subordinate creatures. I like Herder's preaching better than any other that I have heard in my life, but I must honestly confess that I do not like any preaching. The public . . . is much too varied and unequal for his manner to have a generally satisfying unity, and he may not ignore the weak element, as writers do. So what comes out of this? Either he tells the educated everyday truths, or he must confuse ordinary people in order to talk to the educated. A sermon is for the ordinary man – the man of intellect who delivers it is limited, a fantasizer, or a hypocrite.

Thus, two hundred years ago, Schiller, after going to hear a sermon. Had he lived in our days and had he followed Hans Küng, the master of the liberal arts, I am sure that his verdict would have been different: 'By God, the man shows me that as long as one presents the right subject in the right language, in the end it is possible to formulate an intellectual statement that convinces, if not everyone, at least the best from all circles, and not just the religions of Abraham.' That is the success of the thirty-five-year work of a man to whom once a philosopher, Joseph Möller, indicated that he was the right person in the right place. So he was, and will be in the future.

We thank Hans Küng, who has made sure that people all over the world envy us in Tübingen, and in the pantheon of literature where Schiller and Herder embrace each other in divisive harmony and look down on us, we do so even more – as the history of the teacher and orator Hans Küng, the young fundamental theologian and the master with an ecumenical mission, comes to its conclusion – a history which began a third of a century ago in Room 38 of the Tübingen New Aula – and as today, at its climax, the word rings out: 'Work goes on.'

HANS KÜNG

Farewell Lecture

In the winter semester of 1995/96, his last semester at the University of Tübingen as Professor of Ecumenical Theology and Director of the Institute for Ecumenical Research, Hans Küng gave a series of lectures entitled 'Themes of a Lifetime. Theology on the Threshold of the Third Millennium'. The introduction to the whole series ran as follows:

'Themes of a Lifetime.' Certainly also 'Themes of My Lifetime'. So are these lectures about biography? No, but they are about autobiographical theology. Of course doing theology autobiographically is a dangerous undertaking. The suspicion might arise that this theology is less about God than about a quite particular person, his passions, his achievements, his successes. In other words, the suspicion might arise that here at the end of my thirty-six years of theological lecturing at this university I was less concerned with 'theo-logia', with God's truth, than with justifying myself, with demonstrating that in the great dispute over God and the world, the dispute over the truth, I was always right.

Such an impression could not be more fatal. This farewell series of lectures is not meant to be either an attempt at personal justification or an anticipation of memoirs, to be published as soon as possible. Here I am concerned simply to present orally a quite personal account of my own theological standpoint on the threshold of the third millennium, a survey of my past theological work with a view to offering a programme for the future. My concern is with the great themes of theology – as reflected in the themes of my life. I cannot ignore the fact that, as a believing, thinking, hoping human being, from the beginning I have been passion- ately involved in the way in which I have experienced and done theology. Nor do I want to. However, our concern will not simply be 'my' truth, but an account of God's truth, an account of the hope for which the Christian message has laid the foundations in me.

Indeed I am not a little moved that I have been given this undeserved opportunity, and that in this series of lectures I can now once again think through the great themes of Christian theology critically and self-critically with you. And I am deeply moved to see so many young faces here in the hall. They remind me of so many generations of students who have gone on coming to my lectures over past decades and who have kept my own spirit young and open to what is new. They also remind me of my own time as a student when, like most of you, I was completely ignorant of what lay ahead. I could never have dreamed of the way I had to take. I now know that this way resolved itself for me between the ages of eighteen and twenty-eight, and I am sure that this will also be the case for many of you here. In so many eyes I see the expectation of a word of guidance: how can one be authentic, how can one find ground under one's feet? How can one achieve a standpoint? The decisive thing here is to remember that Christian theology does not produce any truth but lives by God's truth, which always comes to life only when it is spoken afresh in truthfulness.

The following lectures were then given:

> *The Basis of Human Existence*
> *The Inescapable Question of God*
> *Orientation on Jesus Christ*
> *Church, Council and Reform*
> *The Possible Unity of Christianity*
> *Peace Between the World Religions*

The text of the last lecture in this series appears below. It is Hans Küng's Farewell Lecture, given at the University of Tübingen on 22 January 1996.

Here, now, is my last lecture, but not my last 'appearance' at our university. Of course my theological work will continue undiminished: one can even travel more lightly without the rucksack of teaching responsibilities. The main direction will be the one I shall be talking about this evening, 'Peace Between the World Religions'. I want first to tell you how I encountered Judaism and Islam, and the consequences that this had for my theology; unfortunately there will be no time for me to say anything about the religions of Indian and Chinese origin.

The first encounter: Judaism

My first encounter with members of a strange religion was completely uncomplicated and natural. The house on the town hall square of our small country town of

Sursee, right next to ours, belonged to the prosperous Jewish textile merchant Leo Heymann, who was a friend of my grandfather (with two others they met every week on Sunday afternoons to play jass). This friendship carried on from the seniors to the juniors and from the juniors to their juniors, and it is still there today. Somehow one took it for granted that this highly respectable family were not Christians; one knew that they did not accept Jesus as the Messiah. What a pity for them, one thought, but otherwise Judaism was neither a challenge nor a problem, either negatively or positively. When in the 1930s a young Heymann went into the lake and drowned while skiing, the whole village was shaken.

Unlike my German colleagues of my generation, even during the Second World War from the beginning I had Jewish fellow-pupils at my grammar school in Lucerne. We all accepted them quite naturally and were only struck by the fact that they did not come to school on Saturdays. There was no animosity on either side, but we did not grapple with any questions of faith or religious practice either. However, what about the Holocaust? We young Swiss learned something about the monstrous discrimination and violation of this people from our press above all in the last years of the war; but it was not until after the war that the full dimensions of this genocide became evident to us.

Nor did we young people have any inkling of how many primarily Jewish refugees had been turned back at our Swiss frontier. Certainly, during the Second World War neutral Switzerland accepted around 300,000 refugees for longer or shorter periods. But above all after 1939, the asylum policy became increasingly strict – out of fear of Hitler's unpredictable anger and the constant threat of a German invasion. Certainly great figures from German literature, art and culture were allowed over the frontier at that time: not only musicians like Hindemith and Bruno Walter, painters like Kirchner and Kokoschka, philosophers like Ernst Bloch ad Rudolf Pannwitz, literary critics like Hans Mayer and Alfred Kerr, and finally writers like Brecht, Döblin, Thomas Mann, Musil, Silone and Zuckmayer . . . When the war ended on 8 May 1945, Switzerland was housing more than 115,000 refugees.

However, in the period from August 1942 to 1945 alone, almost 10,000 primarily Jewish refugees were turned back at the frontier, and countless were deterred from even approaching it. It was said that no more Jews could be allowed into the country; the excuse which was extraordinarily popular with many Swiss was that the 'boat' was full. And this slogan made them politically blind to the desperate needs of the Jewish people. I personally only came to learn this in more detail after 1967 as a result of the courageous but depressing account by the Swiss journalist Alfred A. Hasler of *The Swiss and the Refugees 1933–45*. It was only in 1995 that a member of the Swiss federal government could finally bring himself to make an official confession of guilt on this matter.

In 1948 – the year in which the state of Israel was founded – we left school, Christians and Jews together, and I went to Rome. At the Pontifical Gregorian University I heard hardly anything about the Jewish people – apart from the usual Old Testament lectures. Living Judaism was never communicated to us rising Catholic clergy in Rome as a relevant factor, either politically or theologically. Indeed the people of Israel had been completely superseded by the church of Christ and Jerusalem had been replaced by Rome: that was the traditional Catholic view which was completely taken for granted by our teachers. It took the *Church Dogmatics* of the Protestant theologian Karl Barth to open my eyes, as a Catholic student of theology during my last years in Rome, at least to the theological explosiveness of the theme and the undeniable dialectic of synagogue and church.

However, in all my seven years in Rome I did not hear a word about Christian complicity in the persecution of the Jews and even in the Nazi Holocaust. Was not Pius XII the *Pastor Angelicus*, the greatest pope of the century? Only in Paris, when I made contact with Jewish scholars at the Sorbonne, did it become clear to me that this pope who was so admired had failed in a decisive situation, as a result of his silence. This man, who made more public statements on every possible and indeed impossible question than any other popes of this century, kept quiet here. Not only Jews, but also Catholic Christians, especially the Poles, had expected a clear statement from Pius when the German army invaded Poland in 1939. But this pope, who was in Castel Gandolfo at the time, was not prepared to make one at the outbreak of the Second World War. As the 'father of all Christendom', a title which he was so fond of giving himself, how could he take sides like that? Only at the end of his pontificate did people speak more openly of what he had failed to do, something that was incomprehensible, given that he was a Christian who formally claimed to be the 'Representative of Christ'. Moreover that was the time of Rolf Hochhuth's 'tragedy' of 1963. Here Catholic protests outside the theatre in

Basel were inappropriate. In retrospect I find it even more incomprehensible that after the war the same pope not only suppressed his error but further compensated for it by authoritarian measures against dissidents within Catholicism, especially in France. It is in keeping with this that Pius XII refused diplomatic recognition to the young democratic state of Israel right up until his death in 1958. But the turning point between Christianity and Judaism was to come.

From persecution and contempt to the bond with Israel

Despite or because of my many positive experiences, at that time I still did not have sufficient theological or political awareness of the kind of problem posed by what is called – in a very misleading way – 'the Jewish question' Moreover my 1960 book on the Council was addressed solely to the Christian ecumene. There was no mention of a possible ecumenical co-existence with Jewish brothers and sisters. It was only when a Rabbi Wolff from Chicago attacked me vigorously in public after the appearance of the American edition of *The Council and Reunion* that I woke up. Rabbi Wolff had to tell me that the Fourth Lateran Synod in the high Middle Ages (1215), which I had praised as a reform council, had already enacted most of the discriminatory regulations directed against the Jews which the Nazis were subsequently to implement in a highly organized way: distinctive clothing, a ban on holding public office and on going out on Good Fridays, a compulsory tax, and so on. Only now did I become aware of the terrible history of relations between Christians and Jews. I was thirty-five years old. I decided as soon as possible to investigate this question thoroughly, both historically and theologically.

It was the time of the Second Vatican Council, and John XXIII, that unforgettable first ecumenical pope, had signalled a new attitude of the Catholic Church to the Jews by altering the Good Friday prayer *pro perfidis Judaeis*. To me, too, as a Council theologian working above all with American theologians and bishops, the significance of this question for my own church became increasingly clear. Moreover a Council Declaration on the Jews and on Religious Freedom was then being worked on.

However, the voles in the Curia opposed to this declaration proved successful. And they were supported not only by bishops from the Arab countries but presumably also by influential circles outside the Council. An extremely critical situation developed. I remember the day very precisely: it was 6 October 1964, a Friday. One of Cardinal Bea's secretaries had made it known to our small circle of council theologians and bishops that Paul VI had yielded to political pressure from outside and from the Curia and through the General Secretary of the Council, Pericle Felici, had transferred both the Declaration on the Jews and the Declaration on Religious Freedom from the Council to a special commission.

It was clear to me what that meant, so along with my friends I decided to embark on a counter-offensive. This was the only time when I deliberately violated the 'Council secrecy' which still applied at that time, in order to explain personally to the most important newspapers in the world – from *The New York Times*, *El Pais*,

Il Messaggero and *Le Monde* to the *Frankfurter Allgemeine Zeitung* (which then, unlike today, supported church renewal) – about these scandalous goings-on. The very next Monday, the news was on the front page of all these newspapers. At the same time, through Joseph Ratzinger, with whom I was then on friendly terms, I had drawn the attention of Josef Frings, the cardinal of Cologne, to the seriousness of the matter. On the Sunday evening Frings gathered together the cardinals of Utrecht, Munich, Vienna, Montreal, Bourges, Lille, Chicago and St Louis to draft a letter of protest to the pope with the opening words *magno cum dolore*.

Under the impact of the storm in the press and the letter from the cardinals, the Declaration on the Jews was finally rescued, along with the Declaration on Religious Freedom; it was even considerably expanded within the framework of a special Declaration on the Non-Christian Religions. Granted, in the end a number of points in it were toned down somewhat as a result of intervention from the Curia (antisemitism was no longer 'condemned', but 'lamented', and such like). But despite everything, the Declaration *Nostra aetate* no.4 marked an epoch-making change in the relations of the Catholic Church with Judaism: from persecution and contempt to a recognition of the indissoluble bond between Israel and the church. However, there was not a word in this declaration about living Judaism, and the Vatican, which in this century had made pacts with every possible totalitarian regime in Italy, Spain, Germany and Portugal, did not extend diplomatic relations to the democratic state of Israel until three decades later.

Meanwhile I had studied the history of Judaism in Christianity thoroughly for my book *The Church*, and

Hans Küng

had come to a conclusion which oppressed me: 'We may wonder how this centuries-long history of horrors, of suffering and death, culminating in the murder of millions by the Nazis, could come about . . . ' And in seeking to discover the motivation for this, something became clear to me that I also noted in my stocktaking of the Second Vatican Council in 1965: 'National Socialist antisemitism would have been impossible had it not been for the centuries of anti-Judaism in the Christian churches.' It was this sentence which earned me my first serious rebuke, though still in the form of a personal letter, from the then president of the German Conference of Bishops, Cardinal Julius Döpfner of Munich. Since I had already worked out the whole chapter on 'The Church and the Jews' for my book *The Church*, I sent it to him in manuscript as a reply. It met with a telling silence.

In the year when *The Church* was published (1967), two years after the end of the Council, I went to Jerusalem for the first time. All the hustle and bustle around the birthplace in Bethlehem and the tomb in Jerusalem did not prevent me from gaining a deep impression of the people, countryside and places of work in which the Jew Jesus of Nazareth, who for Christians is the Christ, lived, fought and suffered. Meanwhile I had already been long aware that it is impossible to make 'the Jews' – even 'the Jews' of that time – responsible for the death of Jesus, as the Gospel of John does. In fact, only the religious and political establishment and the Roman forces of occupation were guilty of it. I have already described in previous lectures my conversation with a young European Jewish woman in Jerusalem, what might be called the 'hour of birth' of my personal

80

perspective of a 'christology from below', and the origin of my *On Being a Christian*.

I had now put to myself all the questions Jews ask about our christology, publicly in direct confrontation with the Jewish theologian Pinchas Lapide (our 1976 radio dialogue was brought out as a book), with whom I was later to hold a seminar and in 1989 to give four dialogue lectures, and finally in the first volume of my trilogy 'On The Religious Situation of Our Time', under the title *Judaism* (1991). In the first part of this book I discussed the past which is still present; in the second, the challenges of the present (from the Holocaust to the State of Israel); and in the third, the possibilities for the future.

The future of Judaism

In *Judaism* I attempted to depict Judaism not as a past 'Old Testament' but as an independent entity with an amazing continuity, vitality and dynamism. Here it becomes evident how in Judaism, this oldest of the three great prophetic religions, all the religious problems of our age on the threshold of the new millennium are focussed as by a magnifying glass. All the great religions today are faced today, in the transition to a new world era (post-modern or whatever), with similar structural problems; all are caught up in the basic conflict between tradition and innovation which must be settled and resolved in our transitional period.

It is therefore also particularly important for the Christian or Muslim observer to know whether Judaism will succeed in keeping in view its great centre, its religious substance, and making it comprehensible to a new generation in the midst of all the differences and conflicts, all the various trends and schools, all the battles between Orthodox, Conservative and Reform Jews. What we need in this connection is a Christian and Muslim theology of Judaism within the framework of an Abrahamic ecumene. We no longer need an apologetic which believes itself to be in the right and which is ultimately interested in the disappearance of Judaism, but rather an attitude of solidarity which shares in the good and ills of another religion, the spiritual renewal of which it seeks to further.

But what are the centre and foundation of the Jewish religion? What is its abiding basic structure? According to the Hebrew Bible there is no doubt about this. For whatever criticisms, interpretations and reductions may arise out of historical, literary or sociological criticism, in the light of the normative foundation documents of faith which have exercised such influence down through history, the central content of faith is the one God Yahweh and the one people Israel. There can be no Israelite faith, no Hebrew Bible, no Jewish religion without the confession, 'Yahweh is the God of Israel and Israel is his people!' God's people and land – that characterizes Judaism, just as Christianity is characterized by God's Messiah and Son.

But isn't this a dangerously particularistic and nationalistic standpoint? No, this centre of Jewish faith must always be seen against the horizon of the Hebrew Bible, which is by no means exclusive, but universal. For this is the legacy of Judaism to humankind:
- that God is not just a tribal God but the creator of heaven and earth, of all human beings, races and nations;

- that the first human being is not the first Jew but 'Adam' = 'the human being';
- that the first covenant after the flood was concluded with Noah and thus with all of humankind, and that this happened before the Abrahamic covenant with Abrahamic humankind, even longer before the Sinai covenant with the people of Israel.

Indeed the Noachic covenant has been made with the whole of creation, without distinction of race, class, caste or even religion. Its symbol is the rainbow arching over the whole earth, which bears witness to God's all-embracing rule, reliability and grace. However, this is a covenant matched on the human side by a clear obligation: granted, here we do not yet have specific laws for a particular people, as we do later, but we do have basic requirements imposed on the whole of humankind for its preservation. In other words, the covenant with humankind is matched by an ethic for humankind! We can describe these ordinances of preservation as a minimal basic ethic of reverence for life: not to murder ('for God has made human beings in his image') and not to eat the flesh of animals which are still alive. In rabbinic Judaism five further 'Noachic commandments' were later derived from these two obligations: the prohibition of stealing, fornication, idolatry and blasphemy and the command to cherish the law. So here already we have the biblical basis for a global ethic, all the consequences of which we are only beginning to realize today. Thus the abiding basic substance of Jewish religion must always be seen against this universal horizon, though at the same time it is clear that historically this substance had constantly to be reinterpreted in new epoch-making constellations. The community of faith stood for the proclamation of faith, reflection on the faith and a life of faith in the face of ever new demands, shifting paradigms. So far there have been five of these paradigms, if we survey the more than three thousand years of Jewish history, and now we are evidently in transition from a modern to a post-modern paradigm.

For since the Holocaust and the State of Israel, and facing the new post-modern epoch, like the other religions Judaism sees itself confronted with the dilemma of fundamentalism or secularism. Schematized rather sharply, the alternatives can be sketched out as follows:

- Fundamentalist Orthodoxy strives for a Judaism in religious isolation: a preservation of the religious substance as far as possible without any relationship to the world. By contrast, a radical secularism is nothing but a Judaism emptied of religion: a worldly life without any religious substance.
- Fundamentalist Orthodoxy still lives in a mediaeval counter-world. It is characterized by a legalism that is fixated on Torah and halakhah. By contrast the radical secularists have created a modern substitute religion for themselves: often an Israelism, fixated on survival after the Holocaust.
- In the case of fundamentalism the threat is one of a mediaeval ghetto in which Judaism again isolates itself from the modern world as shaped by Christianity; in the case of secularism the threat is of a modern vacuum in which Judaism diffuses itself in the pluralistic-individualist modern world and threatens to disintegrate.
- In the face of these alternatives, looking towards a post-modern ecumenical paradigm in an ecumenical spirit and referring to contemporary Jewish authors, I

argue for a renewed Judaism in which the various Jewish trends, confessions and denominations do not exclude one another but converge and communicate. Such a post-modern Judaism would be neither a secularistic assimilated Judaism nor a fundamentalist reactionary Judaism; it would be a religiously renewed Judaism. It would again relate the abiding religious 'substance' to the changing world in a new way.

Its religious centre ('essence') would be the same as that of the original Jewish religion: Yahweh the God of Israel and Israel his people; the liberation from Egypt and the revelation of the Torah on Sinai, in a word the covenant, would remain a fundamental point of reference in history. The biblical texts would remain identical, but their interpretation would be variable. The future theological discussion might concentrate on the three difficult questions of whether the law is to be understood literally or not; what is the Jewish character of the State of Israel; and how we can talk of God after the Holocaust.

If Judaism was my first encounter in the world of religions, Islam was the second. And if Judaism can boast of being the oldest and most venerable of the three prophetic religions, Islam can claim that it is the youngest and last and therefore – as Muslims are firmly convinced – the best and most perfect of religions.

The second encounter: Islam

In my young years Islam was not an issue in and for Europe; it was also unknown territory at the grammar school. Even at the Gregorian one heard of Islam only in dry and derogatory statements: that it denied the divinity of Christ and demoted Jesus to a mere prophet. Nevertheless, a fellow student (Franz Knapp) and I were allowed to make a first trip to Muslim countries in 1955, the last year of our studies in Rome. So we went by ship to Tunisia and by train to Algeria, both of which were still a long way away for central Europeans. I have vivid memories of a nocturnal conversation under a bright starry sky on the roof of the neo-Gothic cathedral of Carthage, once the seat of the great metropolitan Cyprian and a place where Augustine often stayed. We talked with the then provincial of the White Fathers, who was reponsible for the Catholic mission to Muslims throughout North Africa. Why, we asked him, had it been impossible to make any progress whatsoever in decades of mission to the Muslims? We were told that the dogma of Christianity was very complicated and that its view of marriage and sex was very rigorous for African Muslim circumstances. The Provincial was now going to withdraw all the missionaries from Islamic Africa and transfer them to black West Africa. When I returned to Carthage last year the Catholic cathedral had become a very fine city museum; there was no longer any trace of Christian missionaries, nor of Augustine's episcopal see in Hippo Regius, called Bône by the French and today known only under the Arabic name of Annaba, where we celebrated Easter Eve in 1955.

In the subsequent period I came to know Islam in the gigantic area from the Atlantic and Central Asia to the Sea of China and the Indonesian islands. Here was an Islam which, in contrast to the views of many anxious people today, is by no means a monolithic entity, a 'green flood' that is once again surging against the shore of Old Europe – if it is not stirred up, as is now happening in the Caucasus. Islam is no more a monolithic unity than Judaism and Christianity. And just as Judaism and Christianity have so far undergone five epoch-making transformations (paradigm shifts), so too, in other, shorter periods of time, has Islam.

What enormous differences there are in Islam, which I came to know in very different countries at very different times:

– In Tashkent, the capital of Uzbekistan, where Russification was already far advanced, Islam was of course completely dominated by the Soviet dictatorship, but it enjoyed more respect and consideration from the Soviet authorities than the Russian Orthodox Church, which they deliberately provoked.

– The situation in Afghanistan, further south, on the 'roof of the world', beyond the Pamir, was very different. Here at that time Islam was still living in peace and freedom. And I was struck by the way in which a well-known Islamic professor there was already acknowledging to a small group that the Qur'an was both the Word of God and the word of the Prophet. At the same time, however, he conceded that he would have to emigrate if he said such a thing publicly; and meanwhile he has emigrated.

– Islam was different again in Lahore in Pakistan, with its splendid Badshahi Mosque, where Islam is the state religion, with all the attendant advantages and disadvantages. Or again, only a short distance from Lahore, in Amritsar in India, at that time one could still visit without any permit the Golden Temple, the central sanctuary of the Sikhs, set in a lake, which was later to become a centre of religious revolt. Here as

87

everywhere in India Islam is a minority, and nowadays more and more Muslims are emigrating to Pakistan.

– Islam is different again in Indonesia, which in its toleration represents the opposite pole to the strictly orthodox Islam in Saudi Arabia or in Khomeini's Iran. I first came to know Iran only very much later, when Saddam Hussein, at that time still encouraged by the West, was dropping isolated bombs on Teheran and other Iranian cities. One fell only a few hundred metres away from me and my colleague Josef van Ess in Isfahan, at eleven o'clock in the morning, producing a gigantic cloud of dust.

All the theological discussions which I was able to have with Muslim scholars in Teheran in 1986/88 and in Riyadh in 1990 would certainly have been impossible without that historical shift which the Catholic Church had made with the Second Vatican Council in its attitude to Islam, as in its attitude to Judaism.

From confrontation to dialogue

The encounter between Christianity and Judaism was overshadowed by persecution: in the Jewish Christian paradigm there was first the persecution of the Christians by the Jews, but then after Constantine in the Greek Byzantine paradigm, and even more in the Roman paradigm of the Middle Ages, the suppression and finally the persecution of the Jews by the Christians. But the encounter between Christianity and Islam has been overshadowed by political and military confrontation between these too religions which are so intimately related and yet so intimately hostile to each other. The first two confrontations developed from the Arab offensive against Byzantium and then the conquest of North Africa and even Spain; the third was the roll-back in the Crusades (which ultimately failed); the fourth was the Ottoman expansion in the Balkans almost to Vienna; and finally the fifth, again in the opposite direction, was caused by European colonialism, which brought almost all the Muslim areas from Morocco through North Africa, Egypt and the Middle East to India and Indonesia under its economic, political and military control. This 'Christian' West, now superior in every respect, is the trauma of Islam which still has not healed, because up to the eighteenth and nineteenth centuries Islam had always regarded itself as a religion of the victors and of victories because of its apparently unstoppable expansion.

But why could Western colonialism and imperialism force to its knees an Islam which in the early Middle Ages was excessively strong in military, political, economic and even cultural terms? Only because since the advent of European modernity, Western science, technology and industry had simply left behind an Islam which had remained in its mediaeval paradigm. So Islam was thrown into an identity crisis which has not yet been overcome. After the First World War and the decline of Islamic supremacy, of the Ottoman empire and the Sultanate, under the aegis of the European colonial powers, there was a territorial reordering of the whole Islamic world from Morocco to Indonesia which only after the Second World War led to these largely newly-founded Muslim nations becoming independent states as a consequence of the process of decolonialization, thus indirectly also leading to a revival of Islam. Since then a war has been raging in the Islamic world over the right course to take between modernization and re-Islamicization.

A whole decade before the oil embargo of 1973, followed by the victory of Ayatollah Khomeini over the Shah and the Americans, which helped Islam everywhere towards a heightened awareness of itself and its power, the Second Vatican Council had achieved a real breakthrough towards an understanding between Christianity and Islam. That is attested by a brief but rich conciliar text which amazingly met with far less opposition than the text about the Jews.

– First, it stresses what the two religions basically have in common:

The Church has also a high regard for the Muslims. They worship God, who is one, living and subsistent, merciful and almighty, the Creator of heaven and earth, who has also spoken to men. They strive to submit themselves without reserve to the hidden decrees of God, just as Abraham submitted himself to God's plan, to whose faith Muslims eagerly link their own.

Then it carefully addresses the main difference:

Although not acknowledging him as God, they venerate Jesus as a prophet, his virgin Mother they also honour, and even at times devoutly invoke. Further, they await the day of judgment and the reward of God following the resurrection from the dead. For this reason they highly esteem an upright life and worship God, especially by way of prayer, alms-deeds and fasting.

Finally, practical consequences are drawn from this reorientation:

> Over the centuries many quarrels and dissensions have arisen between Christians and Muslims. The sacred Council now pleads with all to forget the past, and urges that a sincere effort be made to achieve mutual understanding; for the benefit of all men, let them together preserve and promote peace, liberty, social justice and moral values.

The strength of Islam

The question arises: will Islam preserve its centre in its identity crisis, or will it finally become worldly, a development of which there are already signs? Here a decisive role is played by the way in which the Qur'an, the book which is now the centre of Islam, is understood. Not the Prophet, but the Qur'an is the origin, source and decisive criterion for all Islamic faith, action and life. It has supreme and absolute authority. And not only Western theologians but also Western sociologists, political theorists, philologists and historians must first take seriously the quite specific meaning that the Qur'an has in the life of the masses of believing Muslims. Whenever I heard the cries of prayer and verses of the Qur'an recited from the minarets in Fez or Kairouan, in Cairo, Amman, Riyadh, Teheran or Jogjakarta (sometimes all too early in the morning), I realized what a strange fascination this holy book of the Muslims can evidently have. This is a living book, which does not lie in a cupboard like a family Bible that is used only rarely or is only to be read silently. It is a book which, with the rhyming prose of its Surahs, is to be recited in public time and again; its words and sentences accompany the Muslim from the hour of prayer in which the Qur'anic confession of faith is sung in his ears to the last hour of his life.

But what is this Qur'anic confession of faith? There cannot be any doubt about this either. The unambiguous confession of faith *(shahada)* is of the one God, the almighty and merciful creator and judge, and applies equally to Muhammad, his last and best messenger, even if the well-known confession in a pointed bipartite form, 'There is no God but God, and Muhammad is his Prophet!', does not yet appear in the Qur'an. Together with this simple and at the same time universal confession of faith, which is tied neither to a people nor to a land, the duty of daily prayer, a tax for the poor, fasting and the great pilgrimage to Mecca are the five pillars on which the house of Islam is built. These are its central structural elements or basic characteristics. Since my first visit to North Africa, one of the great strengths of Islam has seemed to me to lie here, in its clear theoretical and practical structuring. The considerable power of integration inherent in Islam is grounded in the compactness of its faith. And whether one has theological discussions with Muslims in Algiers, Lagos, Dar-es-Salaam, Teheran or Toronto, the talk always gets round to the dogmas that Muslims find 'contrary to reason', of one God in three persons and an incarnation of God, statements of faith which make Christian faith so 'complicated' for many people.

Now, at any rate, what these three prophetic religions, so similar and yet so dissimilar, have in common and what divides them is clear. What they have in common is faith in the one and only God of Abraham, the gracious and merciful creator, preserver and judge of all human beings. What divides them is that for Judaism Israel is God's people and land; for Christianity Jesus Christ is God's Messiah and Son; and for Islam the Qur'an is God's word and book.

It seemed to me important to develop theological research into the foundations of the three religions particularly on these three controversial points, which are as central as they are difficult. So in the summer semester of 1982 I engaged in a series of dialogue lectures on Islam, Hinduism and Buddhism (together with Josef van Ess, Heinrich von Stietencron and Heinz Bechert). Here for the first time I attempted to develop a particular method of theological dialogue. In the case of Islam I started with three points from the Vatican II declaration:

1. For Muslims Islam can be the way to salvation. The axiom 'outside the church no salvation' was in fact already abandoned by the Council, but still has to be formally corrected. Unfortunately the World Council of Churches even now does not see itself as being in a position to correct the claim that salvation comes only through Christianity; it is threatened with massive blockages by fundamentalists.

2. The Qur'an can be understood as the Word of God for Muslims, though Christians will always ask whether this Word of God is not at the same time a human word, the word of a prophet, like the Bible.

3. Muhammad, whose name and person are unfortunately not mentioned in the Declaration of Vatican II, can be accepted as an authentic prophet, though at the same time (like all prophets) he had his human limitations and weaknesses. That raises a question.

Hans Küng

The future of Islam

In all this we must remember that quite unlike other prophets Muhammad is a prophet and statesman at the same time; the Qur'an is both a prayer book and a law book; indeed, Islam is a way of salvation and a social system in one. In fact Islam is a system of rules which intervene and regulate down to the last detail of life. That also makes many Muslims ask, where they are free to do so, 'Can Islam also be a "total way" for the whole of economic, intellectual, cultural, social and political life, revealed by God in a new century? Can this be true of the commandments of God – a comprehensive "system" extending down to details, in which religion is utterly mixed up with economics, politics and culture?'

Islam – in comparison to the European development – also seems to many Muslims still to be trapped in its mediaeval paradigm. In other words, Islam – very like Roman Catholicism before the Second Vatican Council – faces a double paradigm shift: not only that of the Reformation, but also that of modernity, the Enlightenment. It faces a tremendous leap from the Middle Ages through modernity to post-modernity. Will it succeed?

At any rate people ask, 'Who will finally gain the upper hand politically – in legal sciences and jurisprudence, *Umma* and state, science and society? Who will be the true heirs of a great religion and culture which is 1400 years old?'

– Will it perhaps be the orthodox traditionalists who – unconcerned with any of the developments in science, law and society – call for a literal application of the detailed religious regulations of the Shariah to the pre-

sent economic and social order and in fact fix this order to the mediaeval paradigm: an Islamic defensive culture with a totalitarian character at the price of self-isolation, further rigidification, alienation from itself and a pre-programmed industrial decline?
– Or will it perhaps be the innovators in both religion and politics who – with a clear perception of the paradigm shift which has taken place in the West – while maintaining the great tradition *(taqlid)* call for an opening of the door of independent interpretation *(iqtihad)* which has been closed since around 900, and attempt a translation (in every sense of the word) of the originally Islamic message to the present day in order to make possible a competitive economy, science and society?

This, I think, is the fateful question for Islam, and it is both political and theological at the same time. Since the nineteenth century it has also been a political question for many open Muslims, say in Istanbul, Egypt and India. Will it ever be possible to combine 'Islam' and 'republic', tradition and modern democracy (this is now again a question in Palestine)? Or will Islam, although theoretically committed to Muslim brotherhood, in practice nevertheless remain authoritarian? Will it remain a kind of theocratic state in which there is no government independent of the clergy and there are no independent parties? A state in which freedom of faith and conscience, the right to resist and legal opposition, are not granted? Where women are denied the right to make individual and political decisions? Where the state knows no religious or ideological neutrality, non-Muslims occupy only the position of a tolerated minority, and only male Muslims have human rights in the modern sense, if anyone does?

Open Muslims are aware that at the same time, and even primarily, for Muslims this is also a theological question. Here the problem arises whether Holy Scripture is to be interpreted literally or by independent responsibility. Here we have the question of the nature of the foundation documents of Islamic faith:

- Must an unconditional divinity and therefore perfection, infallibility and immutability of the 78,000 words of the Qur'an (but indirectly also those of the Prophet's Sunna and the Shariah generally) be maintained?
- Or, as in the case of the Bible, may the historical character of the divine revelation (God's word in the word of the prophet, God's word attested by the human word) be taken seriously?
- Depending on the answers to these questions, the praxis will be either interpretation according to the letter or interpretation according to the spirit. There will be either a religious heritage overgrown with legalism or a religious heritage purged by the criteria of primal Islam.

Identity in modernity, modernity in identity – also to many Muslims today this seems the ideal to be striven for. And just as many Catholics do not want to see a second papal re-Catholicizing of Europe in the style of Wojtyla in place of an ongoing conciliar *aggiornamento*, so too many Muslims do not want an Islamicization of modernity rather than a modernization of Islam. A truly renewed Islam would not need to confirm itself again by confrontation with other cultures and religions.

However, the question of religious confrontation

needs to be raised here quite generally. And much as I would have liked, had I had the time, to go on to speak of my encounters with the religions of Indian and Chinese origin, a general question seems to me to be more important. Are we not facing a war of civilizations? And are not the religions playing more of a negative role here? World peace through peace between the religions – is that perhaps a naive slogan?

A war of civilizations?

The thesis put forward by Samuel P. Huntington, Director of the Institute for Strategic Studies at Harvard University, of a 'Clash of Civilizations?', has been widely discussed. He argues that the wars in a new world era will no longer be wars of nations, as in the nineteenth century, or wars of ideologies, as in the twentieth century, but primarily wars of civilizations. So in future political, economic and military conflicts are to be expected, say, between Islamic civilization and the West, or Confucian Asiatic civilization and the West: 'The next world war, if there is one, will be a war between civilizations.'

I have discussed Huntington's thesis, for which of course much supporting evidence can be found in the contemporary world situation, in my book *Christianity. Its Essence and History*. Here I need say no more than that as a substitute for the scheme of First, Second and Third Worlds, the great civilizations seem to me to be far less able to provide a basic framework on which future world-political controversies can be orientated; here both civilizations and conflicts of all too different origins and characters are systematized. The Arab countries

alone are too different in interests and constitutions for
me to be able to envisage a major conflict between them
and the West, which in any case is vastly more powerful. Can one completely dismiss the suspicion that
Huntington, an adviser to the Pentagon for many years,
who understands little about religions but had a share
of responsibility for the strategy of the Vietnam war, is
looking for a new theory to support calls for armament
and finance for it?

What seems to me true is that in territorial controversies, political interests and economic competition, while
ethnic and religious rivalries are not the dominant factor, they do (as in former Yugoslavia) provide the ideological foundation, the often latent and often virulent
sub-structures by which political, economic and military
conflicts can be justified, inspired and sharpened at
any time. The civilizations or – less misleadingly – the
religions thus form a constant cultural depth dimension
for all political and social antagonisms and conflicts
between peoples, which in no way must be neglected. I
have already been fighting against such neglect in socio-
logy, political theory and practical politics for a long
time. I recently found welcome confirmation of my view
that the religious dimension is being neglected in foreign
policy in a volume produced by Douglas Johnston and
Cynthia Sampson of the Center for Strategic and
International Studies, Washington, entitled *Religion.
The Missing Dimension of Statecraft* (Oxford University
Press 1994). It has many illuminating case studies.

That also allows us to answer the question, 'What
would be the alternative to the threat of a clash of civilizations?' I want to put my reply in a wider context, but
cannot develop it at length here. I shall sum up my

views in four guidelines which aim at achieving the
same results in the macrosphere of world politics as I
attempted in the microsphere of education at the time
of the celebrations for the establishment of the Global
Ethic Foundation. My comments will round off all the
topics that I have discussed.

The alternative: world peace through dialogue between the religions and a global ethic

For reasons of time, here I can only sketch out some
basic statements and develop the guidelines on which
my future work will be orientated:

1. We live in a world and a time in which we are now
seeing new and dangerous tensions and polarizations
between believers and non-believers, church members
and secularists, clerics and anti-clerics, not only in
Russia, Poland and East Germany, but also in Ireland,
France, Spain, Algeria and North America.

My response to this challenge is my first guideline:
There will be no survival of democracy without a coalition between believers and non-believers in mutual respect.

But many people will say to me, 'Don't we live in a
period of new confrontations?' I grant that.

2. We live in a world and a time in which humankind is
threatened by new ethnic-religious conflicts in issues
great and small. However, we are not threatened by a
new world war, but rather by every possible kind of
conflict: between countries or in one country, one city,
even in a street, a school, a family.

My response to this challenge is my second guideline:

There will be no peace between the nations and civilizations without peace between the religions.

But some people may ask, 'Isn't it the religions in particular which so often inspire and legitimate hatred, enmity and war?' I grant that.

3. We live in a world and a time in which peace in many countries is threatened by every possible kind of religious fundamentalism, Christian, Muslim, Jewish, Buddhist or Hindu, a fundamentalism which is often less rooted in religion than in social misery, in reaction to Western secularization and in the need for a basic orientation in life.

My response to this challenge is my third guideline: *There will be no peace between the religions without a dialogue between the religions!* Peace (*shalom, salam, eirene, pax*) is a central feature in the programme of most religions. Their first task in our age must be to make peace with one another. By every means, including those now offered by the media, in cases like former Yugoslavia priority must be given to implementing measures which create trust, specifically:

- clearing up misunderstandings,
- working on traumatic memories,
- dissolving hostile stereotypes,
- coming to terms with conflicts caused by guilt in societies and individuals,
- breaking down hatred and destructiveness,
- reflecting on what is held in common,
- offering positive models.

But many people will object, 'Aren't there so many dogmatic differences and obstacles between the various religions which make a real dialogue a naive illusion?' I grant that.

4. We live in a world and a time in which better relations between the religions are often blocked by every possible kind of dogmatism and infallibilism. This can be found not only in the Roman Catholic Church but in all the churches, religions and ideologies.

My response to this challenge is my fourth guideline; *There will be no new world order without a world ethic, a global or planetary ethic.* One last time, it has to be said that such an ethic for humankind is not a new ideology or superstructure. It does not seek to make the specific ethic of the different religions and philosophies superfluous. Nor is it a substitute for the Torah, the Sermon on the Mount, the Qur'an, the Bhagavadgita, the Discourses of Buddha or the Sayings of Confucius. The one global ethic does not mean a single global culture, far less a single global religion. In positive terms, a global ethic is quite simply the necessary minimum of shared human values, criteria and basic attitudes through which humankind can survive.

A global ethic has become particularly urgent in a world which has become secular, which is characterized by pluralization of the truth and individualization of life: a minimal fundamental consensus concerning binding values, irrevocable standards, and fundamental moral attitudes, which can and should be affirmed by all religions despite their dogmatic differences, and to which indeed non-believers and those of other faiths and views can and should contribute. In the present worldwide crisis of orientation in which all constantly defend their own rights against those of others, often presenting them as human rights, Gandhi's saying is very true: 'The Ganges of rights rises from the Himalaya of duties!'

It is therefore extremely important, not least in order to gain an ethical basis for the long-term responsibility which we are required to show to coming generations and to nature, to study the document which for the first time in the history of religion has formulated such a minimal ethical fundamental consensus between the different religions: the *Declaration toward a Global Ethic* passed by the Parliament of the World Religions in Chicago on 4 September 1993. It was subscribed to by the Dalai Lama along with the Cardinal Archbishop of Chicago, by rabbis and leading Muslims, by Buddhists and Hindus, and also by representatives of countless small religions. I must emphasize what I said right at the beginning of this semester once again at its end: for me the acceptance of this document which I drafted is something like an unexpected 'seal' on my theological activity for the ecumene, both inside and outside the church.

But have I not been able to do much good work also within the Roman system? Theology so to speak first for the pope and thus also for the church and the world? A Catholic colleague asked me this question after the first series of lectures. I have put such questions to myself for a longer time and more frequently than you might think, since as you now know, I did not grow up as an opponent of the Roman system. To conclude, here too I will give you a plain answer.

Two ways

In his memoirs, Yves Congar, the French conciliar theologian (who finally even became a cardinal), describes a private audience with Pope Paul VI. On this occasion the pope told him that the Roman Curia urgently needed capable younger men and here he had thought particularly of Küng and Ratzinger. However, Küng did not seem to have enough 'love for the church'. What the pope told Ratzinger personally I do not know, but I still remember precisely what he told me.

Briefly, just before the end of the Council, on Thursday 2 December 1965, around 12.15 p.m., I was on my way to a private audience with Paul VI. The friendly way in which the Swiss guards greeted me, recognizing me as one of them, and how as I went through the rooms adorned with precious works of art there was a mysterious tinkling (I was accompanied by members of the Cameriere della Spada) belong in my memoirs, and not in these lectures. Paul VI, who, as I knew from earlier encounters, seemed much more sympathetic and warm in personal interviews than on his public appearance, had evidently thought carefully how to guide the conversation. To begin with he extravagantly praised my unusual *doni*, 'gifts'. He remarked that they would enable me more than anyone else, except perhaps my Tübingen predecessor Karl Adam, to advocate Christian truth beyond the *mura della Chiesa* (the walls of the church), and that was important. I began to feel flattered; after all, this was the pope talking to me. But all at once Paul VI made a surprisingly abrupt shift: having surveyed all that I had written, he commented, he would really have preferred me to have written nothing at all.

'*Niente*' – that is not exactly an encouraging compliment from the supreme head to a young Catholic theologian!

The pope said, with a slightly ironical laugh (he laughed in the way that the Caesars must have laughed at poor writers), that he supposed I would now write a good deal about freedom in the church. However, all this was presumably only psychological preparation for the nub of the matter: 'How much good you could do,' the pope said emphatically, 'if you would put your *great gifts at the service of the church: nel servizio della Chiesa!*' I replied gently and with a laugh, '*Santità, io sono già nel servizio della Chiesa*', 'I am already in the service of the church'. But in good Roman style, by 'church' Paul VI had meant the Roman Church, and he continued like this. If he came to Tübingen and walked through the streets there he would first of all also meet many unknown, closed, dark faces, but these would light up when he got to know them better. That was also the case in the Roman Curia. I need by no means agree from the start with everything that happened there. But I had to be prepared – and here the pope's hands made a gesture of bringing into line – to adapt at little. To adapt – that was the issue, and for someone like me who had been educated in Rome, what it meant was quite clear. It was possibly clearer to me than to the non-Roman Ratzinger, who evidently went on to take the way offered to him by the Pope, with not a little success.

You will understand that after this experience I asked myself, 'Should I then perhaps have decided as the pope wanted me to? The chance of a lifetime – did I waste it?' I told myself, first, that I could have done a great deal of good in the Roman system; I will not dispute that. And secondly, that I could have taken the other course at any time. Moreover Paul VI – unlike his successor's successor – blocked any disciplinary measures against me with a note in my file, *'Procedere con carità'* (deal with lovingly). Indeed, shortly before his death, as I learned personally from Cardinal Šeper, the then head of the Congregation of Faith, he had to consider what he, the pope, must do 'to win Küng over'. This must be said in his honour – peace be to his memory.

But during and after that papal audience in 1965 I had become aware that if I wanted to go on doing theology, then I should not do theology for the pope, who evidently does not want my theology as it now is, but rather that in particular I have to do a theology which people can use, after the model of the one who did not say 'I have compassion for the high priest' (though he also deserved compassion) but 'I have compassion for the people'. Hence from then on my programme has been 'theology for my fellow men and women'. That was my way, and down the years I have often quoted the title and song of an early Bing Crosby film, who played a young minister who was also not completely assimilated, 'Going my Way'.

Well, ladies and gentlemen, you have now spent six or seven evenings with me revisiting various stages of my life. You have traced its great themes with me: fundamental trust and the basis of human existence; the criticism of religion and belief in God; belief in Christ and discipleship of Christ; the Catholic Church, the Council and reform; ecumenism and the future of Orthodoxy and Protestantism; and finally, this evening, world religions, world peace and a global ethic. Perhaps you can now understand if I tell you that I could not have gone another way, not just for the sake of freedom, which has always been dear to me, but for the sake of the truth. I saw then, as I see now, that had I gone another way, I would have sold my soul for power in the church. And I can only hope that my contemporary and colleague Joseph Ratzinger, who took the other way and who similarly is retiring this year, is also as content and happy as I am as I look back on my life, despite all the suffering (and I say this without the slightest touch of irony).

After this odyssey, of which I have told you a great deal but by no means all, and which certainly is by no means finished (so you will have to wait for my memoirs!), I can more clearly than ever endorse my *Spero*, which is grounded in my Christian *Credo*. Since I began my theology in Latin, I would now like to formulate it with that brevity of which Latin is so capable. So here is a threefold, not unrealistic, *Spero*:

Spero unitatem ecclesiarum
I hope for a unity of the churches.
Spero pacem religionum
I hope for peace among the religions.
Spero communitatem nationum.
I hope for true community between the nations.

For the future, ladies and gentlemen, all this means that though now I am free from all teaching duties, I shall continue cheerfully, in another way, but hopefully for a long time yet, with all my strength. Thank you for all your sympathy and support, and please continue to show me your good will.

Notes

KARL-JOSEF KUSCHEL

*Theology in Freedom. Basic Dimensions of the
Theology of Hans Küng*

1. Pius XI, *Encyclical Mortalium animos* (1928).
2. Pius X, *Motu Proprio 'Sacrorum antistitum'* of 1
September 1910, English text in J. Neuner and J. Dupuis, *The
Christian Faith in the Documents of the Catholic Church*,
London 1983, 49–51.
3. Cf. H. Küng, *Christianity*, London and New York 1995,
C III: The Roman Catholic Paradigm of the Middle Ages.
4. The basis of this article is the *Festschrift* for the sixty-
fifth birthday of Hans Küng, edited by H. Häring and K.J.
Kuschel, *Hans Küng: Neue Horizonte des Glaubens und
Denkens. Ein Arbeitsbuch*, Munich 1993 (= *Arbeitsbuch*); partial English translation: *Hans Küng: New Horizons for Faith
and Thought*, London and New York 1993 (= *New Horizons*).
5. Romano Guardini got to know the Tübingen dogmatic
theologian Wilhelm Koch during his student days in Tübingen
in 1907/8. Wilhelm Koch was put on the Index in 1916, condemned and thus removed from his chair. For the 'Koch affair'
see M. Seckler, *Theologie vor Gericht. Der Fall Wilhelm Koch
– Ein Bericht*, Tübingen 1972. For the effect on Guardini see
H.-B. Gerl, *Romano Guardini (1885–1968). Leben und Werk*,
Mainz 1985, 52–9.

6. K. Rahner, *Erinnerungen im Gespräch mit M. Krauss*, Freiburg 1984, 81.

7. Cf. P. Hünermann, 'Droht eine dritte Modernismuskrise? Eine offener Brief an den Vorsitzenden der deutschen Bishofskonferenz Karl Lehmann', *Herder Korrespondenz* 43, 1989, 130–5.

8. H. Küng, *The Church and Freedom*, London and New York 1965, 1.

9. P. Sloterdijk, *Kritik der zynischen Vernunft* II, Frankfurt 1983, 522.

10. J. McKenzie, 'Hans Küng on *Infallibility*? This Tiger is Not Discreet', *National Catholic Reporter*, 26 March 1971, reprinted in H. Häring and K.-J. Kuschel, *Hans Küng. His Work and His Way*, London 1979, 79–88.

11. Cf. H. Küng. *Justification. The Doctrine of Karl Barth and a Catholic Reflection*, London 1965. The German edition was reissued with a new foreword: *Rechtfertigung. Die Lehre Karl Barths und eine katholische Besinnung*, Munich 1986, see esp. I-XXII.

12. Cf. W. Jens. 'Mein Freund Hans Küng', in *Arbeitsbuch* (n.4), 820–4.

13. H. Küng, *Freedom in the World*, London and New York 1965, 28.

14. H. Küng, *On Being a Christian*, London 1976, D III, Being Christian as Being Radically Human.

15. For the controversy with Habermas see H. Küng, *Global Responsibility*, London and New York 1991, 41–7.

16. Thus also J. B. Metz, 'Gotteskrise: Ein Portrait der Zeitgenössische Christentums', *Süddeutsche Zeitung*, 24/25 July 1997. Cf. also K.-J. Kuschel, *Laughter. A Theological Reflection*, London and New York 1994, 65–80.

17. H. Küng, *Reforming the Church Today. Keeping Hope Alive*, New York and Edinburgh 1990, 47–8.

18. This is the starting point for Hans Küng's christology, which cannot be developed here. For the basis and development of Küng's christology see my '"Jesus Christ is the Decisive Criterion": Beyond Barth and Hegel to a Christology

"From Below"', in *New Horizons* (n.4), 171–97.

19. There is extensive material on this in *Gegenentwürfe. 24 Lebensläufe für eine andere Theologie*, Munich 1988.

20. H. Kung, *The Church*, London and New York 1967, 136f.

21. Ibid., 253.

22. Cf. J.Moltmann, '"What would a God be who only intervened from outside . . . ?" In Memory of Giordano Bruno', in *History and the Triune God*, London and Minneapolis 1991, 156–64, esp. 158.

23. E. Jüngel, 'Wie frei muss Theologie sein?', *Rheinischer Merkur*, 18 January 1980. Also printed in N. Greinacher and H. Haag (eds.), *Der Fall Küng*, Munich 1980, 383–9: 389.

24. H. Häring and K.-J. Kuschel, 'A call for rehabilitation', in *New Horizons* (n.4), 7–10: 10.

25. This declaration by the Dean of the Catholic Theological Faculty, from which P. Hünermann and H. J. Vogt subsequently dissociated themselves, was reprinted in *Schwäbisches Tagblatt*, 14 February 1996. Already in our *Arbeitsbuch* of 1993, Kurt Koch, then Professor of Catholic Theology in Lucerne and now Bishop of Basel (Hans Küng's home diocese), publicly called for the rehabilitation of Hans Küng as a Catholic theologian. After posing 'open theological questions' to Hans Küng, Koch then wrote: 'Of course these are questions relating to theology, or more precisely to church history and hermeneutics, which do not touch on the Catholic substance of faith in Hans Küng's thought and therefore must – and can – be carried on among theologians themselves. Therefore they are in no way capable of providing legitimization after the event for the condemnation of Hans Küng by the church's magisterium. Rather, they amount to pressure towards a revision of the church's disciplinary measures against him so that the Catholic rehabilitation of the Christian Hans Küng and his theological work take place during his lifetime. What happened to Pierre Teilhard de Chardin, who was only reinstated after his death – albeit hesitantly and not without further posthumous accusations against his person – should not and

must not happen to Hans Küng. In heaven – Christians may rightly be bold enough to hope – Hans Küng will be rehabilitated anyway, along with that chuckling laugh which Karl Barth was convinced was the characteristic of the angels. It is also to be hoped, however, that even during his lifetime Hans Küng may again be granted official recognition by the church as a Catholic theologian and – as a presupposition – again be rehabilitated by Rome' (102f.). We may hope that now as Bishop of Basel, Karl Koch the theologian will intercede even more persistently in Rome for the rehabilitation of Hans Küng.

26. Küng, *The Church* (n.19), 300f.

27. Cf. the monumental study by F. Heer, *Die dritte Kraft. Der europäische Humanismus zwischen den Fronten des konfessionellen Zeitalters*, Frankfurt 1959.

28. K. Barth, *Gespräche (1959–1962)*, ed. E. Busch, Zürich 1995, 124.

29. Ibid, 379.

30. For the complex of problems relating to 'evangelical Catholicity' see the extremely informative study by R. Becker, *Hans Küng und die Ökumene. Evangelische Katholizität als Modell*, Mainz 1996, with a foreword by Hans Küng, which started as a dissertation.

31. This article by Jüngel was published in highly abbreviated form in *Die Zeit*, 26 January 1996. Here I am quoting from the original manuscript version.

32. Cf. H. Küng, 'Christian Revelation and World Religions', in *The World Religions in God's Plan of Salvation*, ed. J. Neuner, London 1967, 25–66.

33. Cf. Küng, *On Being a Christian* (n.14), A III: The Challenge of the World Religions.

34. Cf. H. Küng et al., *Christianity and the World Religions. Paths of Dialogue with Islam, Hinduism and Buddhism*, New York 1986 and London 1987.

35. This basic notion of an ecumenical theology of the world religions in solidarity was first formally expressed in the introduction to H. Küng, *Judaism*, London 1992. He

Notes

stated: 'All these questions already show that here Christian theologians have no certainties, and do not merely interrogate other religions about "their" problems from outside in cold objectivity. Rather, Christian theologians are in the thick of processes of spiritual change and have come to understand that *all the great religions* face *similar structural problems* in the transition to "postmodernity" (or whatever term one uses for the new age) . . . Thus to perceive a global, ecumenical responsibility involves seeing one's own problems better from the way in which they are reflected by others, and passing these experiences on further in resolving conflicts within one's own religion' (xvi).

36. D. Sölle, *Meditationen und Gebrauchstexte*, Berlin 1969, 13.

37. H. Küng, *Theology for the Third Millennium. An Ecumenical View*, New York 1988 and London 1991.

38. H. Küng, *Infallible? An Enquiry*, London and New York 1971, 24.

39. Cf. Kuschel, *Laughter* (n.16).

40. Quoted by Küng at the end of his Erasmus Essay 'Ecumenical Theology between the Fronts', in *Theology for the Third Millennium* (n.37).

Bibliography

Books by Hans Küng in English

Christian existence

Justification. The Doctrine of Karl Barth and a Catholic Reflection, New York: Thomas Nelson 1964 and London: Burns and Oates 1965

A Dignified Dying (with Walter Jens and others), London: SCM Press 1995 and New York: Continuum Publishing Group 1995

The church and the Christian ecumene

The Council and Reunion, London: Sheed and Ward 1961, US title *The Council, Reform and Reunion*, New York: Sheed and Ward 1961

Structures of the Church, New York: Thomas Nelson 1964 and London: Sheed and Ward 1965

The Living Church. Reflections on the Second Vatican Council, London: Sheed and Ward 1963, second edition *The Changing Church. Reflections on the Progress of the Second Vatican Council*, London: Sheed and Ward 1965, US title *The Council in Action*, New York: Sheed and Ward 1963

The Church, London: Burns and Oates 1967, reissued Search Press 1971, and New York: Sheed and Ward 1967

Truthfulness: The Future of the Church, London and New York: Sheed and Ward 1978

Infallible? An Enquiry, London: Collins 1971, second edition SCM Press 1994, and New York: Doubleday 1972

Reforming the Church Today. Keeping Hope Alive, New York: Crossroad Publishing Company 1990 and Edinburgh: T. and T. Clark 1990

Theology and the foundations of christology

The Incarnation of God. An Introduction to Hegel's Theological Thought as Prolegomena to a Future Christology, Edinburgh: T. and T. Clark 1987

Does God Exist? An Answer for Today, London: Collins 1980, reissued SCM Press 1991, and New York: Doubleday 1980

On Being a Christian, London: Collins 1977, reissued SCM Press 1991, and New York: Doubleday 1977

Eternal Life? London: Collins 1984, reissued SCM Press 1991, and New York: Doubleday 1984

Credo. The Apostles Creed explained for Today, London: SCM Press 1993 and New York: Doubleday 1993

Great Christian Thinkers, London: SCM Press 1994 and New York: Continuum Publishing Group 1994

The world ecumene

Christianity and the World Religions. Paths of Dialogue with Islam, Hinduism and Buddhism (with Josef van Ess, Heinrich von Stietencron and Heinz Bechert), New York: Doubleday 1986, reissued Orbis Books 1993 and London: Collins 1987, reissued SCM Press 1993

Christianity and Chinese Religions (with Julia Ching), New York: Doubleday 1989 and London: SCM Press 1993

Bibliography

Art and music

Art and the Question of Meaning, New York: Crossroad Publishing Company 1981 and London: SCM Press 1981

Mozart. Traces of Transcendence, London: SCM Press 1991 and Grand Rapids: Eerdmans 1992

The religious situation of our time

Theology for the Third Millennium. An Ecumenical View, New York: Doubleday 1988 and London: HarperCollins 1991

Judaism, London: SCM Press 1992 and New York: Crossroad Publishing Company 1992

Christianity. Its Essence and History, London: SCM Press 1995 and New York: Continuum Publishing Group 1995

Islam (in preparation)

A global ethic

Global Responsibility. In Search of a New World Ethic, London: SCM Press 1991 and New York: Crossroad Publishing Company 1991

A Global Ethic. The Declaration of the Parliament of the World's Religions (with Karl-Josef Kuschel), London: SCM Press 1993 and New York: Continuum Publishing Group 1994

Yes to a Global Ethic, London: SCM Press 1996 and New York: Crossroad Publishing Company 1996

Books about Hans Küng in English

Hans Küng, His Work and His Way, ed. H. Häring and K. J. Kuschel, London: Collins 1979 and New York: Doubleday 1980

Küng in Conflict, ed. L. Swidler, New York: Doubleday 1981

Bibliography

Robert Nowell, *A Passion for Truth. Hans Küng: A Biography*, London: Collins and New York: Crossroad Publishing Company 1981

Hans Küng: New Horizons for Faith and Thought, ed. Karl-Josef Kuschel and Hermann Häring, London: SCM Press and New York: Continuum Publishing Group 1993

A full bibliography of Hans Küng's writings will be found in this last book, pp. 367–85.